"In my daily life as a Columbia professor, I'm constantly trying to explain to students why a passionate love for learning doesn't necessarily translate into doing graduate work in the humanities. I am incredibly grateful to Kio Stark for this wonderful book that explains the matter much better than I could myself. I intend to put it into the hands of everyone I know who wants to pursue a life of learning but isn't necessarily well suited for a life inside the academy."

—Jenny Davidson, author of *The Magic Circle* and
Breeding: A Partial History of the Eighteenth Century

"Kio Stark's appreciation of real learning over formal education is particularly inspiring at a moment when the cost of a decent grad school far exceeds the lifetime salaries of the professionals it graduates. As a lifelong learner myself, I don't envy those who will never experience at least a few years in the safety and camaraderie of a college campus—but thanks to this engaging book and Stark's enthusiasm, I have new faith in our ability to transcend the quads and forge new academic frontiers."

—Douglas Rushkoff, author of *Present Shock: When
Everything Happens Now*

"The most important learning revolution today is not the open-sourcing of massive online courses by major universities—although that is certainly useful. The most important learning revolution today is the kind of independent-yet-social learning that digital media and networks afford. School—brick-and-mortar or bits-and-bytes—is no longer the exclusive purveyor of learning. But technologies and networks are only effective to the degree that people know how to use them. That's where Kio Stark's *Don't Go Back To School* is potentially more valuable than any 100,000 student online course. Humans are natural learners and school is not only not the sole gateway to learning, it often dulls and sedates our natural thirst for learning. Through examples of successful independent learners, Stark gives us a practical and inspiring vision of how to go about learning in an environment where co-learners, rich curricular materials, and abundant, free, or inexpensive information and communication tools are available."

—Howard Rheingold, author of *Net Smart: How to
Thrive Online* and *Smart Mobs*

DON'T GO BACK TO SCHOOL

A Handbook for Learning Anything

KIO STARK

16.16

Cover and book designed by Ian Crowther/Familiar Studio
Edited by Mandy Brown
Copyedited by Krista Stevens
Cover photo by David Gonsier

ISBN 978-0-9889490-0-3

DontGoBackToSchool.com

Greenglass Books
With support from Gus Rojo and Christopher Warnock

Photo credits

Quinn Norton, p. 22, © Jesse Vincent

Rita J. King, p. 28, © James Jorasch

Brad Edmondson, p. 34, © Kristine Larsen

Dan Sinker, p. 38, © Janice Dillard

Benjamen Walker, p. 46, © Dorothy Hong

Dorian Taylor, p. 52, © Julie Karey

Molly Danielsson, p. 56, © Mathew Lippincott

Astra Taylor, p. 64, © Deborah DeGraffenreid

Jim Munroe, p. 70, © Stephen Gregory

Molly Crabapple, p. 78, © Julianne Berry

Ken Baumann, p. 84, © Jake Michaels

David Hirmes, p. 88, © David Hirmes

Christopher Bathgate, p. 94, © Christopher Bathgate

Caterina Rindi, p. 102, © Troy Sandal

Jeremy Cohen, p. 108, © Andreas Serna

Simone Davalos, p. 112, © Scott Beale

Harper Reed, p. 120, © OFA

David Mason, p. 132, © Jonathan Opp

Karen Barbarossa, p. 152, © Howard Pyle

Cory Doctorow, p. 158, © Paula Mariel Salischiker

Kio Stark, p. 206, © Bre Pettis

For Nika Stark Pettis

Introduction 1

Interviews

Introduction

School is broken and everyone knows it. Public schools from kindergarten to graduation have been crumbling for decades, dropout rates are high, and test scores are low. The value—in every sense—of a college education and degree is hotly contested in the news every day. Students face unprecedented debt in an economy with a dwindling middle class and lessening opportunities for social mobility. This has a significant effect on lives and on the economy itself. The student debt crisis reaches through every facet of people's lives. It affects the housing market as grads with debt are likely to be refused for mortgages, the auto industry as they put off buying cars, consumer spending in general, and decisions to start families. After college, grad school can seem like a refuge from the weak economy, which piles up further debt without clear returns. College students who go on to graduate school also delay the dilemma of the weak job market by using their continued student status to dodge familial pressure to succeed economically. They do this even as it becomes clearer and clearer every day that degrees may not increase their likelihood of getting a job.

This book is a radical project, the opposite of reform. It is not about fixing school, it's about transforming learning—and making traditional school one among many options rather than the only option. I think all the energy and money reformers spend trying to fix school misses the real problem: we don't have good alternatives for people who want to learn without going to school, for people who don't learn well in school settings, or for those who can't afford it.

Because while you don't have to go to school to learn, you do have to figure out how to get some of the things that school provides. Since most of us grew up associating learning with traditional school, we may feel at sea without school to establish an infrastructure for learning. This consists of things such as syllabi to show us an accepted path, teachers to help us through it, ways to get feedback on our progress, ready-made learning communities, a way to develop professional networks that help with careers later, and physical resources like equipment and libraries. In its best and most ideal form, school provides this infrastructure.

But not very many people get to go to school in its best and most ideal form, and my research shows that many learners feel they do it better on their own. People who forgo school build their own infrastructures. They create and borrow and reinvent the best that formal schooling has to offer, and they leave the worst behind. That buys them the freedom to learn on their own terms.

I speak from experience. I went to graduate school at Yale and I dropped out. I had been amazed that I was accepted, and even more so that I was offered a fellowship. Surely this was the fast track to something impressive. But leaving all that behind, to my great surprise, was one of the easiest decisions I've ever made. A gracefully executed quit is a beautiful thing, opening up more doors than it closes. I had invested long years and a lot of work in the degree I walked away from, but I also had innocently misguided reasons for wanting it in the first place. I was fresh out of college and my only thought was that I wasn't done learning.

Nobody had told me that liberal arts graduate school is professional school for professors, which wasn't what I wanted to be. Here's what my graduate school experience was like: I took classes for two years and learned one thing. It was not a fact, but a process. What I learned was how to read a book and take it apart in a particular way, to find everything that's wrong with it and see what remains that's persuasive. This approach is useful to people who are focused on producing academic writing, and it's a reasonably good trick to know, but I could have picked it up in one course. I didn't need two years, and it's pretty annoying to only get to talk about books in such a limited way.

My third year, on the other hand, was bliss. I was left alone for a year to read about 200 books of my choice. I spent that time living far from school in a house in the woods, preparing to demonstrate sufficient command of my field to be permitted to write a dissertation. This was the part of grad school where I really learned things. And for me, what was most significant about the year was that I learned how to teach myself. I had to make my own reading lists for the exams, which meant I learned how to take a subject I was interested in and make myself a map for learning it. As I read the books on my lists, I taught myself to read slowly, to keep track of what I was reading, and to think about books as part of an ongoing conversation with each other. I learned to take what was useful and make sure it was credible and leave the rest aside. I did this with a pen in the margins of the books and by talking to people about what I was reading. I had the luxury of a year to devote to it, but I devour a lot of books even when I'm busy working at a job, and I could have done the same thing over a longer stretch of time. I learned that I didn't need school after all.

Years later, I ran into a young, successful woman who was known for hosting a popular monthly salon on art and technology and for her work as a blogger for a cultural institution. She told me she was toying with the idea of going to graduate school, and wrinkled her nose at the thought. But she lit up when she started describing the things she wanted to study, such as art history and curatorial skills. I reached back to my own hard-won lesson about what liberal arts grad school is really for. I asked her if she wanted to be a professor. She said no. So I asked, "Why do you want to go back to school?" She shrugged a little and said, "Well, I just want to learn things and be smarter about the things I do." That's when I got excited. I had some really useful advice on this, and I got to be the person to tell her about it. You don't need school for that.

—

To someone who has never tried, it's not obvious how to learn the things you want to learn outside of school. I'm on a mission to show you how. To do that, I became obsessed with how other people learn best, and how they do it without going to school. Everywhere I looked, I found people who reach beyond what they're used to, people who create alternatives for themselves and share those alternatives with others. I interviewed 90 of them. As you read, you'll meet 23 of them, people who rejected school early on as well as those who loved school and then graduated into passionate learning without it. They'll tell you how they do it and what drives them to learn.

From their stories, you'll see that when you step away from the prepackaged structure of traditional education, you'll discover that there are many more ways to learn outside school than within. The people I interviewed all touch on similar themes, but they don't all follow the same methods, have the same motivations, or arrive at the same outcomes. As you read on, you'll find a series of complete, complex stories to give you a rich sense of the varieties of human learning experience and help you figure out your own strategies for learning independently.

It's important to say that I interviewed people who learn independently by choice and are happy about it. They've arrived at where they want to be, or feel they're on their way. But not everyone who drops out of school goes on to succeed, and not everyone who tries to learn independently is able to do so to their own satisfaction. There are social and economic reasons for that, and there are individual hurdles that no mere book can knock down. What I can do is solve some significant problems for people who try to learn on their own and haven't been successful. These problems include not knowing how independent learning works, not having any models for success, and not knowing anyone else who is learning independently. I want to ensure that no one ever has to fail at learning on their own for those reasons ever again.

My research revealed four facts shared by almost every successful form of learning outside of school:

- It isn't done alone.
- For many professions, credentials aren't necessary, and the processes for getting credentials are changing.
- The most effective, satisfying learning is learning that which is more likely to happen outside of school.
- People who are happiest with their learning process and most effective at learning new things—in any educational environment—are people who are learning for the right reasons and who reflect on their own way of learning to figure out which processes and methods work best for them.

I'll give you the most critical information about each of these themes in this section, and you'll see them echoed in the interviews and advice that follow.

Learning is something we do together

When I began the interviews for this book, I referred to the people I spoke with as "independent learners," and it's still the most useful shorthand. It's compact, and it suggests the maverick quality we associate with rejecting institutions. The problem is, it's also wrong.

Independent learning suggests ideas such as "self-taught," or "autodidact." These imply that independence means working solo. But that's just not how it happens. People don't learn in isolation. When I talk about independent learners, I don't mean people learning alone. I'm talking about learning that happens independent of schools. Almost all of the people I interviewed talked about the importance of connections they forged to communities and experts, and access to other learners. One of my interviewees said it better than I could: "The first thing you have to do is take the auto out of autodidact."

Anyone who really wants to learn without school has to find other people to learn with and from. That's the open secret of learning outside of school. It's a social act. Learning is something we do together.

Independent learners are interdependent learners. Caterina Rindi worked as a teacher and a nonprofit administrator for years. She wanted to start her own business, and thought the way into that would be business school, but she didn't get in. Undeterred, she joined a "Faux MBA" reading group started by some acquaintances, where she learned everything she needed to start and improve her small business. Likewise, Molly Danielsson, a self-taught expert on composting toilets, formed a salon with other friends and community members in her area who were interested in DIY sanitation. "This has been one of the best things for our design process," she told me.

The internet has always been good for this kind of community-based mutual aid. For years, peers, novices, and experts have been connecting and helping each other on myriad bulletin boards and forums, and on sites such as Stack Overflow or Ask MetaFilter. There are also more recent experiments in facilitating this sort of generosity and openness between experts and novices. For example, a service called Ohours allows anyone to hold online "office hours," making their expertise available to anyone with a question. You'll see many examples in this book of novices and experts connecting and the importance of this strategy for independent learners.

For independent learning to thrive, we need many more tools for opening up education, connecting like-minded learners, and allowing them to reach out to experts. There's a boom in startups experimenting in this area, but most of these experiments are not useful for meaningful learning, and many focus on connecting learners with material, rather than connecting learners with each other, which is a crucial component. Nonetheless, I'm thrilled to see every new development. We need a flood of these experiments. Providing genuinely useful infrastructure for independent learning is a challenge, and good systems are built on the failures that precede them. These platforms and networks will live or die by how well they facilitate participation and collaboration.

The experiments that are currently most well known are massive open online classes, or MOOCs. The MOOCs you'll frequently hear about in the media are offered on platforms such as Coursera, Udacity, P2PU, edX—with new platforms debuting every semester. Their goal is to provide higher education at a massive scale. The field of open online education is quickly changing, and my hope is that it will also quickly improve. And while there are individual teachers experimenting in wonderful ways with opening up their own classes online for mass participation, MOOC platforms are a different story.

MOOC platforms largely replicate school—including traditional school's problems. The professors vary widely in their actual teaching skills and in how engaging they are to students—that capacity for performance that great lecturing requires. Grading is built around tests and quizzes that often contain ambiguous questions, without much feedback on wrong answers. Innovative educators I talked to note that tests are arbitrary motivators and aren't likely to lead to long-term retention of class material. In MOOCs, written assignments are pitched at a relatively low level of difficulty, and there's no way to accommodate students' varying skill levels. These are the very facts about school that most of my interviewees cited as reasons why they didn't like school. Simply put, MOOCs are designed to put teaching online, and that is their mistake. Instead they should start putting learning online. The innovation of MOOCs is to detach the act of teaching from physical classrooms and tuition-based enrollment. But what they should be working toward is much more radical—detaching learning from the linear processes of school.

By contrast, the tools I'm most excited about focus on creating online environments for collaborative learning. One great example that provides a simple, effective system to form groups, coordinate learning, and connect people was developed by Tarmo Toikkanen and his colleagues at the Media Lab Helsinki. The prototype is called TeamUp, a web-based tool for teachers to get students learning in small groups and working as teams. The system facilitates group formation and allows group leaders and participants to monitor progress. It was designed for classroom teachers but can be used by anyone. (The platforms, tools, and experiments I found most promising are listed in the **Resources** section at the back of the book.) If MOOCs were to incorporate tools like these, it would be a giant step in the right direction. Because the most successful learning happens when students are able to communicate and learn together.

It isn't only independent learners who prize their learning communities. When I asked people who did go to school what they liked about their time there, they unanimously cited "other people" as the most useful and meaningful part of their school experience. Artist Golan Levin said school was most meaningful to him for "the community and personal learning networks, and occasions for intellectual stimulation. In other words, side-by-side collaboration and competition with both peers and mentors." Artist and city planner Neil Freeman thrived at a small liberal arts college because of "the proximity to a mass of fellow learners." Challenge, collaboration, and exchanges of knowledge aren't the only reason "other people" are important. They can be examples of different paths in life than the ones you have imagined for yourself. Advertising creative director Ingrid Ducmanis found that exposure to people with different ideas about what's possible after graduation elevated her goals and her notions of how to achieve them:

> It was the people around me who taught me an important thing. I learned a sense of entitlement from rich kids. As a middle-class Midwesterner, being exposed to genuine rich kids from New York and Boston and California opened my eyes to more possibilities and encouraged me to reach for more

than I might have otherwise. I got the idea to move to New York City, to aim for a real career of my own making.

Given the primacy of community in the experience of learning, the question of how to take the auto out of autodidact is the first and most central question for learners. The stories in this book will show you how to find and make communities. Taking the auto out of autodidact is also the central challenge for technology-enabled experiments that aim to facilitate independent learning; the stories here are a map for the success of new learning platforms. Entrepreneurs and developers need to understand the basic dynamics of how people learn without classrooms: What they need in order to do so, and where there are opportunities to make those processes better. We are ready for a world in which people can learn without institutions. Technology gives us networks and tools; conferences and informal gatherings give us learning environments; and we have the desire. It's time to make connecting with others to learn an everyday act, as ordinary as going to school, rather than something done only by an "independent" minority.

Traditional credentials aren't as important as you think

Degrees and careers are no longer as entwined as you have been led to believe. No one I interviewed who had dropped out of school at any level has had a problem making a living in traditional or nontraditional careers. There is a caveat to this—my research has what's called a "sample bias," because the people I interviewed are all happy with their choices and scrappy in their approach to their careers. But for anyone considering the independent path, my interviewees' career experiences are useful and instructive parables for how to negotiate the world of jobs when you don't have traditional credentials.

The independent learners I interviewed all use a variety of strategies for succeeding in their careers without getting traditional credentials:

- They use portfolios to show their past projects and demonstrate competence.
- They show both enthusiasm and "chutzpah," which is an insistent, confident attitude. Similarly, they're willing to stretch the truth a little to get a foothold.
- They are adept at learning on the job, and often choose to "start small." For example, aspiring journalists may take jobs at small local papers.
- They are meticulous about doing good work and being helpful in their workplaces or for their clients. Writer Neil Gaiman offered a perfect model for this in a commencement speech in 2012:

You get work however you get work. But people keep working, in a freelance world—and more and more of today's world is freelance—because their work is good, and because they're easy to get along with, and because they deliver the work on time. And you don't even need all three. Two out of three is fine. People will tolerate how unpleasant you are if your work is good and you deliver it on time. People will forgive the lateness of your work if it's good and they like you. And you don't have to be as good as everyone else if you're on time and it's always a pleasure to hear from you.
See the video at is.gd/leyeva.

■ They use connections from their learning communities to find jobs and get recommended for work. This relies on participating in the economy of generosity in their community, understanding that helpfulness is a two-way street.

You're not crazy if you feel like college and grad school credentials are necessary to your career. To varying degrees, credentials have been increasingly important as higher education opened up over the past 50 years. Until World War II, many good, middle-class jobs remained open to people with high school diplomas. After the war, the GI Bill radically increased the population of college grads by paying tuition for war veterans who were accepted to any school, but the resulting "glut" of college grads upped the ante for many jobs. As higher education became more universal, each step in the educational ladder has been devalued.

Another change since the GI Bill is an increase in the professionalization of previously generalist fields, such as public relations, marketing, advertising, journalism, communications, accounting, and management. These were once fields open to enterprising people with a high school education or a liberal arts degree. Now, you can major in these fields in college, and may have to.

Finally, as a historical trend, people with college or graduate degrees have higher lifetime earnings, a statistic often cited in discussions about the value of education. The problem is that this statistic is based on long-term data, gathered from a period of moderate loan debt, easy employability, and annual increases in the value of a college degree. These conditions have been the case for college grads for decades. Given the dramatically changed circumstances grads today face, we already know that the trends for debt, employability, and the value of a degree have all degraded, and we cannot assume the trend toward greater lifetime earnings will hold true for the current generation. This is a critical omission from media coverage. The fact is we do not know. There's absolutely no guarantee it will hold true.

All of this adds up to a common perception that if you don't have a degree, your résumé won't make it through the slush pile. The good news is that this is starting to change. Given the current turmoil in higher education, it has to. I don't mean that people need less knowledge to do their jobs. I mean that as a culture, we need to—and are starting to—respect learning and competence gained outside of school.

Employers are getting there. Some companies are reconsidering the way they evaluate résumés and credentials, much to the benefit of independent learners. Tony Hsieh, CEO of Zappos, a company known for its innovative approach to business practices, told me, "I haven't looked at a résumé in years. I hire people based on their skills and whether or not they are going to fit our culture." A recent NPR piece reports that instead of hiring exclusively college grads, corporations such as Siemens are experimenting with apprenticeship and training programs for high school grads that lead to guaranteed jobs. Work experience and demonstrable skills, as well as cultural fit with a company's values, are starting to matter more. The way we think about and acquire credentials is also changing. Alternative forms of credentialing, such as certificates for non-institutional and online learning, are beginning to be taken more seriously and are becoming more available, particularly in technical and communications fields.

A few professions are inflexible about the need for official credentials, and that's unlikely to change. These are completely closed to people who don't have a license and the profession-specific degree required to get the license. The most common examples are healthcare professions, law, teaching in a public school, and architecture. In these cases, there's no way around it. These "protected title" professions require traditional educational credentials with no alternatives. If you want a job in one of these fields, you're in for a mandatory dose of higher education.

Other careers don't require licenses, but often seem from the outside that an advanced degree is the only entrée into an elite world with strict gatekeepers. Think of these soft credentials as a way into "culturally closed shops," such as fine arts, fiction writing, sciences, finance, or engineering. While an advanced degree might make some doors easier to open, you can succeed in these fields without the advanced degree. You'll read stories here about people who did just that. I spoke to entrepreneurs and finance professionals without MBAS. I spoke to artists and writers without MFAS and, in some cases, without undergraduate degrees either. I spoke to scientists without PhDs. All of them preferred their independent path and found it more engaging, and more profitable than years spent pursuing a degree.

The last issue related to credentials is how gender factors in the relationship between degrees and jobs. Careers such as journalism, finance, sciences, and engineering have been, historically, men's work, only opening up to women in the last few decades. Women still hold fewer of these jobs, and are battling against long-standing perceptions of gender that often make it such that they have to work harder to get and keep those jobs. This means, for many women, doing things "by the book" seems a more reliable path. If you are already at a disadvantage in the race for jobs, having to forge your own professional networks and demonstrate your competence gets a lot harder. You'll see examples in these interviews with women who have succeeded without going to school, but these hurdles are serious and not to be discounted, whether or not school is an ideal way to learn.

The only good way to learn is to do it your own way

Learning your own way means finding the methods that work best for you and creating conditions that support sustained motivation. Perseverance, pleasure, and the ability to retain what you learn are among the wonderful byproducts of getting to learn using methods that suit you best and in contexts that keep you going. Figuring out your personal approach to each of these takes trial and error. I'll talk here about what each of these factors means, and you'll see them played out in the interviews that follow.

For independent learners, it's essential to find the process and methods that match your instinctual tendencies as a learner. Everyone I talked to went through a period of experimenting and sorting out what works for them, and they've become highly aware of their own preferences. They're clear that learning by methods that don't suit them shuts down their drive and diminishes their enjoyment of learning. Independent learners also find that their preferred methods are different for different areas. So one of the keys to success and enjoyment as an independent learner is to discover how you learn. It will probably involve some frustration and failures. But it will pay off.

Flexibility about your methods is inherent to independent learning. You might prefer a linear path over a path based on discovery. You might prefer to organize your learning around concrete, definable projects. You may find that what really solidifies your learning is teaching others what you've learned. Diving in and learning by doing, on the fly, is a common strategy. Reading and listening are ways of gathering information. You can learn through conversation by participating in communities focused on your area of interest, and by tagging along with people who know more than you. You can talk to experts. And all of these are learning methods you can do together with others.

School isn't very good at dealing with the multiplicity of individual learning preferences, and it's not very good at helping you figure out what works for you. In its most ideal form, it's definitely true that teachers try to cater to more than one way of learning. It's equally true that they don't have the resources to do this on an individual basis, nor the time to make this process transparent to students. So even in an ideal school situation, you probably won't get the most crucial thing, which is learning about the way you learn. If you do figure this out in school, it will probably be by a process of elimination, and that's only if you realize that it's a question you need to answer.

One of the first questions for most people is whether they prefer to learn in a linear fashion, starting at the beginning of a traditional path and following it, or whether they follow a more chaotic and exploratory process. Many of the people I interviewed reported that they worked differently on different kinds of material. Some people drive without directions; some people drive by looking at maps.

For linear learning, school used to be the only place to get access to a map that charted a tried and true path to learning a particular subject. These maps, such as syllabi and textbooks, were scarce, restricted resources. But school is now far from the only place to find these kinds of maps. Open courseware, experimental learning platforms, and the generosity of individual teachers in sharing their work mean that school isn't the only place to find a well traveled path anymore. They're widely available without paying tuition. Good old fashioned textbooks can be found cheaply and easily online. Astra Taylor taught herself math and science on her own and relied on easily available curricula and textbooks along the way: "The fallacy is you can teach yourself arts and humanities but not science. Actually I think it's easier to teach yourself math and hard sciences up to a point. There are right answers and very objective measurements of progress. Textbooks are very linear." This makes massive-scale online learning with services such as Coursera, Udacity, and edX a good strategy if you're inclined toward linear learning. Astra also learned to be a filmmaker by jumping into making a film and figuring it out as she went along. Her story is a perfect example of how you may prefer different processes for different areas of knowledge.

So, linear structure is often a very useful approach, and a prevalent one, especially for people who are new to teaching themselves. But following a map isn't the only strategy for learning. It's equally true that some people thrive on learning without them. Many people I interviewed described jumping in at the point of fascination and working their way in every direction to find what they needed to understand their subject. People who learn this way talk about the value of connections they stumble into along the way—the purposeful feeling they have pursuing bits and pieces in the context of an immediate need to understand something they are strongly motivated to understand, rather than because it's the next chapter in the textbook. Dan Sinker, an editor and journalist with no formal training in these or many of the other jobs he has had, describes his approach to learning new things: "Here's how I start: Run at 100 MPH in one direction, get pretty far and realize I'm in the wrong place, turn around and run 100 MPH in another direction. It's not a great way to learn quickly, but it really does give me a very wide understanding of a problem. Even though backtracking can be really frustrating, I tend to come out with a breadth I wouldn't have if I was a little more methodical about it." Computational biologist Florian Wagner emphasizes the advantages of "a more chaotic path" as a process by which you are "more likely to stumble upon other, unrelated topics that you wouldn't have found out about otherwise, so it keeps your mind open." Learners who operate this way tend to think that separating knowledge into disciplines and depending on the accepted canon of knowledge in each discipline are conveniences for the institutions that house them, rather than tools designed for the benefit of learners.

Reading stories in this book, you'll see how these different approaches, and a host of others, suit different learners in different contexts. You'll have lots of processes to experiment with as you find the way that works best for you.

—

Now let's talk about motivation and sticking with it when you're learning outside the classroom. A lot of people balk at the idea of independent learning because they think it won't work without the structured expectations of the classroom. They subscribe to the idea that having homework, a reading schedule, and regular tests will help you learn and drive you to stick with it. This turns out to be a fundamental misconception about how people learn best and when they are happiest with the experience of learning. School-like online learning platforms such as Udacity, edx, and Coursera, with massive enrollments, also have massive dropout rates. Independent learners describe their aversion to the arbitrary deadlines and forms of evaluation that school offers. They detail their disinclination to stick with school learning and their abiding motivation when it comes to learning things they choose to learn on their own terms.

There is a rich body of knowledge about the psychology of motivation in education, which I explored after I finished interviewing learners. What I read echoed everything I had already learned about motivation by talking to self-educated people about why they are driven to learn and why they stick with it. Learning outside school is necessarily driven by an internal engine. I heard about how this works from people who follow their deep curiosities and immediate needs for knowledge and skills to reach personally set goals. You'll see in the chapters ahead how independent learners stick with the reading, thinking, making, and experimenting by which they learn because they do it for love, to scratch an itch, to satisfy curiosity, following the compass of passion and wonder about the world.

Self-taught scientist Luke Muehlhauser, executive director of the Singularity Institute, describes his own quest for knowledge as based on "genuine curiosity, a burning itch to understand reality," he told me. "If you have that kind of curiosity, it can motivate you to do all the other things that you need to do in order to learn." Karen Barbarossa, a writer, programmer, and interface designer, has several university degrees and can't imagine learning without being driven by her own curiosity. "I think part of why people teach themselves things—why I do—is really for fascination or love or something that drives them to need what they're learning. I've never known what it's like to be uncurious."

Any young child you observe displays these traits. But passion and curiosity can be easily lost. School itself can be a primary cause; arbitrary motivators such as grades leave little room for variation in students' abilities and interests, and fail to reward curiosity itself. There are also significant social factors working against children's natural curiosity and capacity for learning, such as family support or the lack of it, or a degree of poverty that puts families in survival mode with little room to nurture curiosity.

I heard from teenage dropouts who felt that school and its rigid structure were plainly opposed to their desire to learn. Several of my interviewees described how often in high school they would get absorbed with the material at hand, only for the bell to ring, forcing them to switch gears and go to another class. They described a fundamental problem with school learning: It motivates students with external—rather than internal—demands and rewards. These are things such as grades, arbitrary deadlines, and test-based evaluation, with its "correct" answers. There's also competition for artificially scarce rewards such as praise, attention, curve-based grades, and diplomas—and for genuinely scarce resources such as scholarships. Often, this all has exactly the opposite effect that's intended. To the people I spoke with who found school to be a poor learning environment, these motivational structures felt contrived, and pushed inherently smart, curious people to drop out. For filmmaker Charles Kinnane, who dropped out of high school and later got his GED, "the beautiful thing about learning on your own is you have to be motivated about the subject to do it. Anyone can go through the motions at school, but self-learning may be the easiest way to find out what you're good at." Consultant Dorian Taylor, who dropped out of formal high school and has never been to college says, "In my experience, the single most important criterion for learning something is wanting to. Like genuinely intrinsically so. Virtually everything I've learned to satisfy some extrinsic goal has been faddish and empty by comparison."

As Kinnane and Taylor describe, the internal engine of independent learning runs at the opposite end of the spectrum from school's external demands. According to both my interview data and academic research on motivation, three broadly defined elements of the learning experience support internal motivation and the persistence it enables. Internal motivation relies on learners having autonomy in their learning, a progressing sense of competence in their skills and knowledge, and the ability to learn in a concrete or "real world" context rather than in the abstract. These are mostly absent from classroom learning. Autonomy is rare, useful context is absent, and school's means for affirming competence often feel so arbitrary as to be almost without use—and are sometimes actively demotivating.

Let's go through these three elements and see how they work. First, autonomy means that you follow your own path. You learn what you want to learn, when and how you want to learn it, for your own reasons. Your impetus to learn comes from within because you control the conditions of your learning rather than working within a structure that's pre-made and inflexible.

The second thing you need to stick with learning independently is to set your own goals toward an increasing sense of competence. You need to create a feedback loop that confirms your work is worth it and keeps you moving forward. In school this is provided by advancing through the steps of the linear path within an individual class or a set curriculum, as well as from feedback from grades and praise. Outside of school, people I talked to got their sense of competence from many sources. Many reported to me that they often turn around and teach what they've learned to others as soon as they've learned it. This gives them a sense of mastery and deepens their understanding. When their learning is structured around a specific project, successful completion and the functioning project proves their progress. Projects can include making a computer program, constructing a book, making a film, writing about an unfamiliar topic, starting a business, or learning a skill. Projects give you a goal for learning skills and abstract information alike, and contribute to gaining a sense of mastery and competence as you complete them. Feedback and recognition from respected peers supports that sense of competence. Failure was also described as an unexpected key to mastery. For many, to fail and learn from it and then go on to succeed feels like more concrete progress and a deeper learning experience than getting it right the first time.

The third thing can make or break your ability to sustain internal motivation, as described by my interviewees and academic researchers alike, is to situate what you're learning in a context that matters to you. In some cases, the context is a specific project you want to accomplish, which, as mentioned above also functions to support your sense of progress.

My interviewees also described their learning as taking place in a "real world" context "with consequences." Entrepreneur Jeremy Cohen says he used his savings "to experiment in the real world, where it counts." Similarly, novelist and filmmaker Jim Munroe says he "learns the hard way about things often, but I have to, I feel, to internalize it properly." When Molly Danielsson needed to put her desire to learn about composting-toilet design into a context with consequences, she and her partner "decided that to stick with our crazy plan we had to start telling people about it so they'd hold us to it. I know I won't do good work unless I have someone watching me." Danielsson used her community to help keep her on track. These are examples of people learning by doing, in public, with the possibility of failure, and self-imposed pressure to meet their self-defined goals.

There are more abstract subjects that don't immediately lend themselves to purposeful, project-based learning out in the real world. There may also be prerequisites to understanding at more advanced level. If you want to read contemporary philosophy in a deep way, you have to read at least a sprinkling of classical philosophy. Or perhaps you want to learn Medieval history or basic statistics. You may not have immediate needs or use for this knowledge. This is another reason that learning communities are key—when you're learning with people, being prepared to participate in discussions can be reason enough to do the "homework." You can also take a lesson from project-oriented learning, and consider creating useful contexts for yourself: Write a children's book about Plato. Choose a scientific article you're excited about whose methods you need statistical literacy to understand and to decide whether you trust the information. Record a video for YouTube to share your new knowledge of medieval weaponry. Invent a compelling reason that will help you use, share, or teach what you're learning.

School is not designed to offer these three conditions; autonomy and context are sorely lacking in classrooms. School can provide a sense of increasing mastery, via grades and moving from introductory classes to harder ones. But a sense of true competence is harder to come by in a school environment. Fortunately, there are professors in higher education who are working to change the motivational structures that underlie their curricula. For example, when I was looking at the academic research, I spoke with Debbie Chachra, a faculty member at the Franklin W. Olin College of Engineering, an engineering school created in 2002 to educate engineers for the climate of innovation that now dominates their profession. To be successful, her students need to learn flexibility and the ability to adapt and learn on the job. That's not really the focus of the traditional engineering curriculum. Chachra and her colleagues have created undergraduate engineering programs that foster a lot more independent learning: "Teaching closed-ended problems toward the old job model isn't giving students the other skills they need—lifelong learning skills, how to find information, self-direction, how to figure out where to go, and communication skills."

I asked Chachra why fostering intrinsic motivation in a classroom environment is important. She said intrinsic motivation correlates with the most highly prized characteristics of education: Engagement, retention, and active learning. "All evidence shows that people learn better when they're learning with intrinsic purpose. And they're happier too." Studies have proven that people do better at everything—other than purely mechanical tasks—when they're intrinsically motivated. These are crucial facts for formal and informal educators to know about, and employers too, since to be a skilled worker now requires the constant ability to learn and adapt. The benefits of internal motivation are things independent learners know in their bones.

My interviewees, the academic research, and Chachra's comments all support the notion that internal motivation simply works better and can be fostered or halted by the conditions of learning. People who learn this way report a tremendous sense of satisfaction with their accomplishments and in discovering their ability to teach themselves. Computational biologist Florian Wagner speaks for many of my interviewees: "There is something really special about when you first realize you can figure out really cool things completely on your own. That alone is a valuable lesson in life."

The future

Should we just close all the universities tomorrow? No, or at least not yet. A great deal of our advanced knowledge about how the world works and what it means still resides in these institutions, and as a culture, we haven't figured out how to make room for and fund that activity in other ways. Independent learners also depend in part on access to materials generated by schools—video and audio lectures, professors sharing their materials, syllabi, textbooks, research, and scholarly publications. Learning outside of school profits by its ability to borrow from inside schools.

That access is increasing. The publication of high level research, which has been closely guarded, is in a moment of radical transformation. The scholars who publish their research to share it with the world and stake their claim to discoveries are agitating successfully for open access. Currently, most scholarly journals are not available to people who don't have university library access. Subscriptions are prohibitively expensive, and publishers insist that they need to charge those rates to sustain their businesses. The scholars and researchers who write the articles and perform the rigorous "peer review" process to validate the articles are not paid for their work. If they want their scholarship to be freely available, they are asked to pay upward of $3,000 to the journal publishers. Incensed by these conditions, as of this writing, over 13,000 researchers have essentially gone on strike, refusing to participate in the scholarly publishing industry by withholding their work, declining to perform peer review for closed-access journals.

There's no doubt that as things stand we still need research universities. That said, everything about the higher education system as it exists now is up for grabs. It's impossible to predict the ways in which it may change, mutate, reinvent itself, or become obsolete and falter. Right now, learning in and outside of school runs on parallel tracks. I don't know if that will continue, or if alternatives will eclipse the primacy of school-based education. But I am sure of two things: That independent learning isn't going away, and that school's monopoly on learning and the things that enable non-school learning is already crumbling. I'm excited that those things are happening and I'm working to make them happen faster.

For those of you who have experience with learning outside of school, this book is a celebration of what you do. For those of you who haven't, it's a warm invitation to give it a try.

How to use this book

Theories of learning emphasize the idea that we don't all learn in the same way. Hearing from the dozens and dozens of learners—some of whom you'll meet in this book—made that exquisitely real for me. Twenty-three of the most nuanced and insightful interviews follow and will hopefully serve as role models to inspire you. Reading their stories, you will hear how communities facilitate learning, how different learners find their own way, and even how to get a job without credentials. You'll encounter many different learning approaches you can try out for yourself.

If you read the book from start to finish, you'll get an in-depth understanding of how and why independent learning works by seeing it in action in real people's lives. You'll find a wide variety of individual approaches to learning that you can try out to find the ones that suit you best. You'll see the ways people find and form learning communities and why that's beneficial to them. You can also dip in and out of the book where it's most useful to you. Following the stories of people who learned the kind of things you're eager to learn is a great way to get insight into tackling that field or skill outside the classroom. The brief how-to sections are there for you to discover how to build specific pieces of learning infrastructure and get solutions to problems you're having with learning outside school or are worried you might have if you try it.

JOURNALISM

Quinn Norton

"The best way to get someone to tell you what they know is to share your own knowledge, too."

Quinn Norton *is a writer and photographer whose work has appeared in* Wired News, *the* Guardian, Make Magazine, Seed, FAIR, *the* Irish Times, *and other publications. She covers science, technology and law, copyright, robotics, computer security, intellectual property, body modification, medicine, and other topics that catch her attention. She has also worked as a teacher, a stand-up comedian, and a technologist. Quinn has a* GED *and attended college intermittently but did not graduate.*

Quinn is a lifelong practitioner of the "fake it till you make it" approach to independent learning. Here she talks about how she learned the method and how it's served her, as well as the other ways she learns best: by listening, talking to experts, and by teaching formally and informally. She offers insight and concrete advice about learning to evaluate sources of information for quality and bias. Quinn has been successful at getting and keeping a variety of jobs without the usual credentials. As an object lesson, she tells the story of learning to be a journalist on the job, and what it takes to do it well.

My educational experience was categorically terrible. I was thrown out of elementary school, and then high school later on. Throughout my childhood, I escaped from my troubles into a library. So for me, learning things from books was very natural. I didn't learn very well in school and usually I didn't learn very well from my teachers. I ditched high school a lot and went over to the University of California, Los Angeles, and crashed classes.

After I left high school, I started a furniture refinishing business with my mom's help. I learned some really interesting lessons there. My mom taught me to look at any crazy thing that a client was looking for, cross my arms, look thoughtful for a minute, and say, "Yes, I can do that." Then I'd work like mad to figure out how to do it. In that, I learned how to "fake it till you make it," which is a serious life lesson. To make it work, you have to learn to teach yourself fast. But you also have to learn to forgive yourself when you fail.

The furniture business was fine, but it wasn't what I wanted to do forever. I wanted to be a writer, and I wanted to keep learning. Later, I would sneak into University of California, Santa Barbara, classes and listen to lectures. I learned how to learn from lectures. To this day, lectures are one of the best ways I can learn things, now on my iPod. To really get it, I listen to the same lecture back to back, twice. I have a good auditory memory, and then I just discuss what I've learned with whoever is around in order to understand it and make it stick.

I did eventually get a GED, but not until I needed student loans to go to community college. I never took a computer class in college. But I got a job in the library at the computer lab, so a lot of my learning was by teaching other students. I started printing out and reading the technical documents that specify the protocols on the internet. I snuck them into my classes and read them while I was supposed to be reading other things. When you're sneaking around reading this obscure technical stuff, there's something wrong with you. Wrong, but possibly something lucrative and useful.

I ended up teaching that knowledge to others at the school. That's one of my most effective ways to learn, by teaching; you just have to stay a week ahead of your students. I trained staff and faculty about what the internet was, how to use it, and how to write web pages. I also designed a five-week workshop for the more intensively interested people called, "The Internet from the Ground Up." It was a fire-hose blast of everything about the technical core of the internet, the things I'd been sneaking around reading. Everything I learned, I immediately turned around and taught to others.

This was also when I figured out that I could get help from people who had serious expertise. It was easy. At the time, the key to learning things on the internet was mailing lists. If I was interested in something, I'd join the mailing list on that topic. That gave me access to the best people in the field. It was more open in those days, but you can still do this. While I was in school, I was really interested in marine science. I got on the marine mammal research list. I thought I was just going to lurk and learn, but I found out that experts are not actually out of reach to nonexperts at all. Experts are experts because they like their topics. They like talking about them. If you want to talk about them, great. You'll have a much easier time getting an expert in marine mammalogy to tell you all about dolphins than football. If you are genuinely interested in people, it's not that hard to get them to teach you. You do have to do some homework first so that you're asking interesting questions, not totally elementary ones.

At a certain point, I couldn't afford to stay in school anymore. I went to work at a computer sales/service company. We were talking about MIME types, browser cookies, database-driven websites, and all this kind of stuff that was exploding in '95. I had no idea what I was doing. I spent the entire time I was there basically leaning back, crossing my arms, looking thoughtful for a minute, and then saying, "Yes, I can do that," just as I had with the furniture. I spent a few years getting different jobs like that, where I wasn't really qualified, so that I could learn new things.

After a while, I burned out on computers and the internet. I looked in the classifieds and found an ad for a computer teacher for junior high and high school students. I went in and said, I don't have a teaching credential, let's just get that out of the way. So I'm not qualified on an academic level. I phrased that very carefully. They said they'd try to figure out how to hire me without a teaching credential. They just needed to have someone who knew computers really well. I said that I knew computers really well, which I did. A few months later, they figured out I didn't have a college degree at all, or a high school diploma. The principal did a double take. "You didn't ask," I told him.

I was a very odd teacher. This was a computer class, but what I was really interested in teaching the students was how to think critically and evaluate the information they were consuming. I hated grading. I remember standing up in front of them and telling them that grades don't matter. You just need to calm down. Grades do not matter. They just looked at me, blank stares. I told them, in ten years, do you know who's going to care about the grade that you got in this class? No one in the universe. Not even you are going to care about the grade that you got in this class.

One of them raised their hand and asked, "Well then Ms. Norton, what matters?" I told them what you learn matters. The skills that you get are useful.

Not the grade that you get. They were aghast. Everything for them, and for me growing up, was about good grades, getting into college, in order to be a full human being. I hadn't done any of that. Here I was, a full human being, and I was telling them grades didn't matter.

The best thing I did for them was that I taught them basic research skills that applied to both online information and what you get from books. It's about triangulating information. You have to go through a lot of different sources, trying to see what makes sense, asking people who might know, and compare what you find. See who agrees with whom and figure out why. It's both the source and the voice of what you're reading that tell you how to interpret it. You have to learn this by doing it. There's no substitution for practice.

We played a game in class called the Batcave assignment. I put a number of terms into a hat. Weird terms—"ball lightning" was one of them. Conspiracy theories, just bizarre things. All the students had to come up and take a topic out of the hat. I gave them an hour to research it online. Then they did a ten-minute oral presentation on what they'd found. The first five minutes was what they found, the second five minutes was what they thought about what they found.

They learned from practice how to consider the source by looking at how it used language, for example. If you read something on the Centers for Disease Control site, you might trust it more than some possibly crackpot individual's page. So you think automatically the CDC is the authority, but it's not always like that. The source and the voice are important. The CDC might be talking around something, and the crazy page might be a patient telling their experience. That's important.

I ended up quitting teaching because I couldn't get any health insurance. Years later, after being an unqualified systems administrator, a stand-up comic, and a UI designer in the first dot-com boom, I came back to my original ambition to be a writer. It was another case of me doing things without much experience. You can do a lot of things if you're not worried that you're not supposed to be able to do them. I did two articles for the O'Reilly Network. I used those two pieces as credentials and did a pitch to the *Guardian*. They took one of the pieces that I pitched them. The next thing I did was pitch *Wired*, having written for the *Guardian* and O'Reilly Network. They took the piece. So I had three writing credits.

When I wanted to learn something new as a professional writer, I'd pitch a story on it. I was interested in neurology, and I figured, why don't I start interviewing neurologists? The great thing about being a journalist is that you can pick up the phone and talk to anybody. It was just like what I found out about learning from experts on mailing lists. People like to talk about what they know. Working as a journalist, I found the secret for getting people to teach you anything. The best way to get someone to tell you what they know is to share your own knowledge, too. By then I had this peripatetic knowledge set that went all around technology and technological culture and history and even marine mammals. I thought about it as a kind of a trade. I could always leverage something I knew into something I didn't. When I had to interview someone and I didn't understand their area of expertise, I'd read about it. But then I'd also figure out what their interests were. I'm stuffed with trivial, useless knowledge, on a panoply of bizarre topics, so I can find something that they're interested in that I know something about. Being able to do that is tremendously socially valuable. The exchange of knowledge is a very human way to learn. I try never to walk into a room where I want to get information without knowing what I'm bringing to the other person. Once I do that, I'm golden. I may not understand anything about your product or the science you do, but maybe you're interested in old Chinese water clocks, and we can talk about that. I have this sparking little glowing fact I can give you. Or, sometimes that thing I can bring is to be funny and interesting and good company. Sometimes good company is the best thing you can offer.

I think part of the problem with the usual mindset of the student is that it's like being a sponge. It's passive. It's not about having something to bring to the interaction. People who are experts in things are experts because they like learning. So what you've got when you talk to an expert, ideally, are two curious people having a conversation, one of whom is you, and you both know different things you're willing to share. I approach every interview or interaction like this: I'm going to bring you a present, then, I'm going to ask you for a present as well.

Quinn Norton's website is quinnnorton.com

Rita J. King

"*I thought I had to start my career at the center of things, but that turned out not to be true at all.*"

Rita J. King is the Executive Vice President for Business Development at Science House in Manhattan. She currently serves as Futurist at NASA Langley's think tank, the National Institute of Aerospace and is a Global Fellow at the Salzburg Global Seminar, specializing in creative collaboration. Rita is a former investigative journalist on the nuclear industry.

Rita's independent learning has been the mainstay of her education, despite having gone to college. She's a wonderful example of how getting a job isn't tied to having a degree, since she's never discussed her education with potential employers. Her career as a journalist depended on her skills as an independent learner and on the generosity of people she contacted and learned from. She explains the process by which she learned about the extremely complicated nuclear industry in both scientific and political terms.

I have always been an avid learner. I love to learn, but I deeply disliked the feeling of being trapped at school. When I was eight, I spent a day with my father that gave me a roadmap for learning for the rest of my life. He was a disabled Vietnam veteran, and the GI Bill paid for his education at Columbia. Sometimes he used to let me skip school and go with him to college classes. One day he took me to his physics class and I learned about quarks. I was absolutely stunned. Up quarks, down quarks, charm, and strange—enchanting and mysterious subatomic particles. I became obsessed with physics from that moment on. After physics class, we went to French class and watched a film. Thankfully, my parents didn't have any concept of age-appropriateness. All in one day, I got obsessed with art, culture, and science. I've been that way ever since. From then on, all I wanted to do was read physics textbooks and make art. It became even harder to sit through school after that.

In terms of college, my father erroneously assumed that because the GI Bill paid for him, that I would also have a full scholarship anywhere I wanted to go. I worked really hard to make the most of this privilege I was counting on, since it had cost him so dearly earlier in his own life. Turns out he was not correct about the GI Bill, nor had he saved any money to educate me. I was an excellent test-taker and student, despite feeling stuck in school, and I was accepted into all of the universities I wanted to attend. Instead, however, I ended up going to a state school and funding most of it myself because that's what I could afford. After years of being conditioned to believe that anything less than an Ivy League education was completely unacceptable, I was devastated and lost all interest in college. It took every ounce of my self-control to force myself to go. I could have transferred, but I had no desire to accumulate debt, fearing that it might force me to take a job that sucked my soul to free myself.

After I graduated, I wondered if I'd be perceived as less capable or desirable because I didn't have an Ivy League degree. So I tried an experiment. When I looked for work, I didn't talk about my education at all. I approached my career like an adventure, accepting work that led to other work and built on itself. I could have been a PhD from Harvard, or a high school dropout, nobody knew either way. It was a fun experiment to see the assumptions people made about my level of education, and also to see how much other people rely on having been educated at a prestigious university for social capital. There has never been a situation in which I needed to prove that I have a degree to get work. People never ask. I was a journalist. I had my own company. I now work at Science House in Manhattan. As a consultant I've worked with IBM, Manpower, and the National Institute of Aerospace. I've worked all around the world, sometimes in highly academic settings or as a senior fellow at think tanks, and even then the question of where I was educated almost never comes up. The most useful thing I did learn in college was basic human interactivity skills. At a top school, the connections you make help you later. I didn't have that. Because I didn't have that network of connections when I graduated, it made me so much scrappier, and I took a more interesting, adventurous route.

I decided to become a journalist after I saw a book called *The Journey is the Destination*, a collection of the art of photojournalist Dan Eldon who was killed in Somalia in 1993 while covering the crisis there. There were photographs from all over the world. He was so young and vibrant. I was flipping through this book and I thought to myself, this is how a person should live. I was 25, living in Cooperstown, getting ready to move to Manhattan. I had my moving van packed. A friend of mine who was helping me move was curious about Cooperstown, and asked me to pick up a copy of the local paper to see what it was like. I found out they were looking for a reporter. I figured I had to start somewhere, so I walked in to see if they'd hire me. They asked if I had experience, and I said, look, just try me out. I cobbled a portfolio together and they hired me that afternoon. I got an apartment and unpacked the truck. I stayed there for two years as a columnist and a reporter. Like most people, I thought I had to start my career at the center of things, but that turned out not to be true at all. You build skills up and you use them as stepping stones to get to the next thing.

After working for the Cooperstown paper, I again planned to move to New York City. In the meantime, I was staying in Westchester. My first day in town, I ran into a woman who asked me, "Did you get your pills?" What pills? "Potassium iodide pills," she told me. "If there's a radiation leak at the plant..." It turned out we were in the peak fatality zone of the Indian Point nuclear plant. I got a job at the local paper covering Indian Point, figuring I would only work there for a few months. I wanted to know everything. Why did they choose that location so close to New York City? How much power actually needs to be generated and how cheaply? Are there hidden costs? The questions were endless. Fascinated, I stayed for several years.

To learn about something so complicated, it helps to lay it out in pieces. There's the territory that's affected by the thing you're learning about. Then you learn who the key players are, how powerful they are, how much influence they have. I took a holistic view of the tax base of the region. Did supporters support Indian Point because it pays for the school districts around it, for example, and/or because it provides jobs? A lot of math was required to make sense of the reality of the situation. I had to understand the safety and security issues. My life was taken over by trying to understand the interlocking systems involved. When you start to tackle something new, it's tempting to start with the granular details, but for me it's more effective to start understanding the system in which the thing itself operates. Mapping things out is really helpful. Categorizing components and striving to be rational, to overcome natural emotional responses is critical. The nuclear industry evokes fear of danger, but it's so much more complicated than that.

Listening is the best way to learn. I didn't just call activists and citizens on the phone and say, "Tell me about your relationship with the plant." I would sit down with people in their homes. I went to countless meetings. I talked to people who were invested in the industry. I interviewed everyone. Anytime I heard anything technical that I didn't understand, I interviewed as many scientists as I could.

Scientists who work for the industry explain things one way, and scientists who work outside the industry, or have no connection to it, explain things another way. It's important to interview people who are coming from different perspectives, not just to find a pro and a con and call it a balanced piece. You can really just call up people who have expert knowledge. It's up to them to call you back or not. I talked to many scientists who gained their knowledge through years and years and years of formal education. In such cases, formal education is a necessity. That doesn't mean that you have to be formally educated to know what you're talking about, but many of the people I talked to were. Most people I called were eager to talk about what they knew.

When you're learning something, it's really important not only to understand the system and context in which that thing functions, but also to look ahead and imagine what the world would be like with or without this thing. These four years enabled me to create a template that has served my entire career since.

After Hurricane Katrina, I knew that the Waterford nuclear plant in Louisiana was an immediate concern. The power was out, and the plant had been fined by the Nuclear Regulatory Commission because their backup generators, which might have ended up keeping the spent nuclear fuel rods cool during a blackout, had a spotty safety record in the past. I immediately created a blog and posted an open letter to the Waterford plant and to the Nuclear Regulatory Commission asking what they planned to do about the backup generators. An organization called CorpWatch saw this and offered me an assignment to investigate post-Katrina corporate profiteering across the Gulf Coast. Through those investigations, I gained knowledge about the relationship between corporations and the government and how that functions.

My career now centers completely on science, art, imagination, and business. I've learned about these fields through years of immersion. I continue to live and work that way. Life changes constantly, and flexibility is the best path to keeping your skills and perspectives current. Formal education is valuable in the right context but it tends to be rigid, which can put students at a serious disadvantage when they graduate from academia and enter the world. Each person is at a different stage in the learning process. We need to all take a step back and see ourselves on a continuum of the learning experience. I may sometimes have to stop everything I'm doing and put my hand out and pull you up. Then other times, I may have to ask you to stop everything and pull me up. It's the only way for us all to keep moving ahead.

Rita J. King's website is <u>sciencehouse.com</u>

Brad Edmondson

"Learning on the job is basically how any journalist will start—as a cub."

 **Brad Edmondson** *is an independent journalist and consultant who lives in Ithaca, New York. He was cofounder of* ePodunk.com *and the editor-in-chief of* American Demographics *magazine. His writing appears regularly in national magazines, including* AARP *and the* American Scholar. *His focus is on social change in the United States and its influence on businesses and other institutions.*

Brad refers to his many years on the job at a national magazine as "his grad school." He learned the craft of journalism and magazine publishing by walking in the door and offering to work at a local publication. He's a great example of an apprentice route that many journalists take to getting jobs and learning by doing—and how journalism as a profession is an educational pursuit.

I always wanted to be a writer and tell stories. I majored in history, and loved it, and I thought I would be very happy going on to get a graduate degree in history, but the more I learned about the graduate school system the less I liked it. I really did not like the idea of spending the next ten years basically being a slave in one form or another in order to get a job as a historian.

So I became a journalist because it was also a way to get writing experience. My first job was at the *Ithaca Times*, a local weekly. When I started there, I was really green. I had taken one class in school called Basic Newswriting where I learned about the Associated Press manual. I didn't know the nuts and bolts of putting a newspaper together. Learning on the job is basically how any journalist will start—as a cub. You pick up things from people with more experience. You end up as the editor, in my case after two years as a reporter. It was a great way to learn journalism and publication skills because it was a very small operation.

Eventually I needed more money. There was one national magazine that was based in Ithaca and it was across the street from the *Ithaca Times* office. That was *American Demographics*. It was quite prestigious already when I started, and later was a finalist for the National Magazine Award three times. So, I got a job there by offering myself as a stringer without knowing a single thing about the magazine. After being a stringer for eight months, I was hired as a junior editor. The thing about *American Demographics* that was really exceptional was that the editors there, as a group, created a radically new way of writing about social change by integrating demographic analysis with standard reporting techniques. During the 1990s, as computing power got cheaper and software got better, we also lead the way in improving maps, charts, and other graphics that turned statistics into stories. They were really hot, getting a lot of attention and their work was cited in the media all the time. I was on the staff of that magazine for 13 years and it was a really terrific place to work. That's really what I did instead of going to graduate school.

What I got there was real mentoring. The editors who had those skills and taught them to me were all fairly humane and forgiving of mistakes. They wouldn't let anything into print that had a mistake in it. But when they found a mistake in your work, they would correct you and more explicitly expect that you wouldn't make that mistake again. The people I was learning from were also my friends. It was really a social situation for learning and that made it exceptional. People were having fun there. It was like a class that I really looked forward to, and it was my job. I was learning something and getting cited by the *Washington Post* and traveling to New York as an expert.

I left the magazine when it moved to New York City in 1998. There are still only a few journalists who have the analytical skills I learned there. There isn't excessive demand for it, but when somebody wants it, they really want it, and I'm one of the only people they can call. I still make a living doing the same kind of analysis I did there, as a consultant, and also as a public speaker. I couldn't have gotten that work, which is quite remunerative, without the education I got on the job at *American Demographics*.

Brad Edmondson's website is <u>bradedmondson.com</u>

Dan Sinker

"All my pressure comes from within: from hearing about something and wanting to dive further into it, or from having an itch I really, really, really want to scratch."

 **Dan Sinker** *heads up the Knight-Mozilla OpenNews project. He was the founding editor of the influential underground culture magazine* Punk Planet *and is now a self-taught journalist, publisher, and coder. He has no advanced degree, but worked full-time as a professor at Columbia College. Dan authored the popular @MayorEmanuel Twitter account, now collected as a book published by Scribner in 2011. He created an election tracker called the Chicago Mayoral Scorecard, and the mobile storytelling project CellStories.*

I heard from many people that they learned the most by doing projects they loved and learning on the fly, rather than by going to class. Dan has approached learning with this DIY *spirit his whole life. Here he describes his path to becoming a journalist, editor, and publisher, all of which he learned from publishing a magazine he loved. There's a subtle but important point in Dan's story—that skills you learn in one field often become useful in an entirely different pursuit. I loved hearing about the chaotic and exciting process Dan goes through to learn new things, in this case learning what he needed to know to launch CellStories.*

I spent 13 years running *Punk Planet* and a larger publishing company called Independence Day Media. I started *Punk Planet* when I was 19 years old, halfway through college. I was going to the Art Institute of Chicago to study video art. I did finish college, although I almost didn't because I was really involved in the magazine. Like all punk scenes back in the late '80s and early '90s, everyone was so young. The big local bands were comprised of 17-year-olds. Record label people were probably a little younger than that, and the people doing the zines were even younger than that. It embodied everything about DIY ethics that I love: Nobody checking credentials, nobody asking if you have any real skills to do the things that you say you're going to do, and instead really empowering people to do those things.

Moving back and forth from that scene to art school was deeply alienating, because they were about as opposite as you could get. In school, there were a lot of people talking about their ideas and then waiting for some sort of validation before they'd do anything. I didn't feel like I had a lot of peers in school because I was the one actually making things happen. I ended up on the internet all the time and on message boards, where I found people who were involved in their own punk scene and ended up building a little bit of a virtual community. *Punk Planet* magazine grew out of that. So, I was paying money for an education, but at the same time, really feeling like most of the education I was getting was actually happening on nights and weekends. That's when I was with this group of people and none of us knew what we were doing, but we began to figure out how to run a magazine and how to make something like that happen. I thought about dropping out of school a number of times, but I had gotten far enough down the road on my degree that I just felt like I needed to see the thing through. In my last year of college half of my classes were independent study so I could work on *Punk Planet*. That was probably the best use of tuition money.

The first couple of years of *Punk Planet*, it was a terrible magazine. Part of that was because nobody involved knew how to run a magazine. One of the skills we needed to learn was what an editor does. At some point I realized that everything that I had learned about editing video actually applied to editing anything. I can remember that moment very well when I thought, wait a second, I do know how to do this. I just knew how to do it in a totally different way. So I applied what I knew about video to stories in the magazine, and suddenly the magazine transformed. So, that is the one thing that I will credit to my college education. I've barely touched a video camera since I graduated, but it absolutely taught me how to be an editor.

The magazine folded in 2007, and I ended up at Stanford University for a year as a Knight Fellow, which is a fellowship program for mid-career journalists. To me the fact that I got this fellowship based on *Punk Planet* was hilarious. It was probably about five months before the end of the magazine and I was looking for alternative funding. I actually typed "journalism grants" into Google, and the Knight Foundation popped up on the top and in poking around their site, I ended up on the Knight Fellowship page. I thought there was no way that would happen. It was something for Pulitzer winners and very traditional journalists. But my wife and my friends said, why not? It turned out they were in the middle of rethinking their process, and I was one of a few outsiders they brought in as guinea pigs to try a different approach. It was an incredibly lucky thing, to have applied right at that time. I got to just be in a place and have open access to whatever I wanted to do. I mainly looked into what the influence of mobile technology was going to be on culture. But, I've joked many times that if that hadn't happened I probably would have ended up working at Arby's. Instead, after the fellowship, I taught digital tools and strategy to journalists at Columbia College in Chicago. I did that for three years as a full-time faculty member.

Besides publishing *Punk Planet*, the best example of something I learned totally outside of being a student is when I built CellStories.net, which was a cell phone literary magazine that published one story every day and delivered it to your phone. It ran from September 2009 to the end of 2010. Building and running it encompassed tons of different types of learning. It was built from scratch in a framework I taught myself (Ruby on Rails). I developed it around a lot of different theories and ideas on mobile content delivery and consumption. I tend to not learn well from external pressure. All my pressure comes from within: from hearing about something and wanting to dive further into it, or (most of the time) from having an itch I really, really, really want to scratch. In the case of CellStories it was a combination of the two. I really wanted to learn a robust framework for dynamic web creation for a multitude of reasons, and I was super interested in mobile phones and wanted to learn all I could about them. This started back in the fall of 2007, so in the baby steps era of iPhones.

To learn all that, basically I did what I always do. I start running at 100 MPH in one direction, get pretty far and realize I'm in the wrong place, turn around and run 100 MPH in another direction. It's not a great way to learn quickly, but it really does give me a very wide understanding of a problem. Even though backtracking can be really frustrating, I tend to come out with a breadth I wouldn't have if I was a little more methodical about it. And, generally, that breadth becomes helpful eventually. Mostly. To keep everything straight, I live and die by Moleskine notebooks. I fill them with notes, ideas, sketches, names, etc. I tend to have three or so going at any time, one for specific projects, one simply labeled "Ideas," and one or two for classes.

Learning outside school is unimaginable to me without engaging with other people. And lonely. As co-working spaces become more popular, I keep wishing someone would come out with a co-learning space. It's not about a desire for a more structured environment. Just people around to be able to bounce ideas off of, to help you think things through. When I'm looking for people to talk to and learn from, I just hit people up. If I wanted to talk to someone who was doing something interesting in Africa, say—like the people who made the crisis reporting platform Ushahidi—I'd just drop them a line. It is pretty incredible how responsive people are in answering and engaging. I've found that, by and large, people who are passionate about the things that they do are very happy to engage with other people that are passionate about what they do.

There's always this great moment when you really figure out that you've actually learned something, because you suddenly realize that you're doing things that you couldn't do before. Like, for instance, I've been hitting my head against the wall with some JSON-related stuff lately. And suddenly, the other day, without even being at a computer, I figured it out. In my head. And it was so obvious! But it felt great. Those moments keep coming. I had been doing CellStories for about a year and I realized: Wow, I know this stuff now. And then my immediate response was: NOW WHAT?!

Dan Sinker's website is sinker.tumblr.com

GENERAL KNOWLEDGE

Benjamen Walker

"Having public output and public conversations about what I was reading and studying became part of the learning process."

Benjamen Walker *is the host and producer of the weekly radio show and podcast* Too Much Information *heard Mondays 6–7 p.m.* EST *on* WFMU *in Jersey City. He also produced the* Big Ideas *podcast for the* Guardian *and has contributed to shows such as* Radiolab, On the Media, *and other Public Radio programs. He is a college graduate.*

Benjamen describes his college education as a self-guided, DIY *experience that didn't prepare him for the academic career as a philosopher he imagined for himself. He began to work toward gaining a deep knowledge of philosophy by reading and discussing his ideas with peers. This led to his career as a radio producer, a perfect example of the value of sharing and publishing your ideas as a means to learning. Any career that allows you to do this is a great choice for independent learners. Benjamen shares his passion and knowledge in conversation and through his radio work. In doing so, he's created a life of ongoing independent learning.*

I went to public high school and it was horrible. Then I loved college. I went to Montana State University in Bozeman. I had a special experience in Montana because they had an interdisciplinary program that they had just started which allowed you, through the honors program, to make your own degree. So I made my own film theory/film production degree. I just had a blast.

The first day of freshman English class the teacher had us read George Orwell and Charles Bukowski. I felt like my brain turned on that day. It was the other students and teachers who did that for me. They loved reading and literature in a way that I had never been exposed to in public school. I had luckily fallen into this DIY environment. For me, formal education worked only because I had a lot of control over what I was learning. I was basically free to build my own course of study. When I look back, it's very clear that what I was doing was not dependent on school, it was dependent on me. I was interested in lots of things and I made it work for me.

After that, I thought grad school would be the greatest thing in the universe. I was like, if this is school, I'm never leaving! I thought that going into philosophy as a profession would be a great existence. What else possibly could I imagine doing than academia? I decided I wanted to go to the New School in New York and get a PhD in Nietzsche. I even chose the guy I wanted to study with. I had it all figured out. Except that we're talking about thousands and thousands of dollars per minute to go there.

I went to New York and met James Miller, who I wanted to study with. I walked into his office and we talked for a bit and it became very clear to me that without a rigorous study of the German language, I could not be a Nietzsche scholar.

While we were talking—and I will never forget this—he said, "You remind me of a student that I had, that I really loved that was really unhappy. Grad school just wasn't for him and he fell apart." I thought, why are you telling me that?

I went and sat in on a couple of his classes. I wanted to be there so bad. I thought it was going to be so great. After that we went back to his office and talked some more. He asked me about what I was reading, what I was interested in, and then he said, "If you don't go to grad school it's not like you won't keep learning and reading." The overt message I heard was that I wasn't good enough. But the subtext I heard at the same time was incredibly liberating. You don't have to go to school to do the things that you're interested in. It was such a powerful experience and revelation. From that moment on, I never thought of grad school again.

I was free to choose my own approach to engaging with the philosophy I was excited about. The first thing I did was to stop reading secondary literature, the books that are about the actual philosophy and literary books I wanted to read. It was such a cool approach for me. I spent a good year reading classics and contemporary literature and philosophical texts. I ended up reading probably six or seven volumes of Kierkegaard one year and I was thinking: If I was in grad school I would have had to read all of the secondary sources and argue about whose interpretation is right or wrong.

I didn't have the magic box to tell me what to read. So I went to the library a lot and the librarians would point me to various places. I talked with friends and people who were also interested in similar subjects. I ran into things all the time that I didn't understand. Partially I got through that by talking to other people. But also I think that so much of what I'm interested in philosophically is precisely about what's not understood and the journey of grappling with that. I would be worried if I was able to understand everything.

I was setting my own goals and expectations of what I wanted out of something or why I stuck with a certain thing. When I wanted to move on to a new writer or subject, I always questioned myself. Am I done or am I worried I don't have the intellectual capacity for that? I tried not to change reading paths because of that worry, to make sure I pushed myself.

Around the same time that I got started with self-study, I got involved with radio, and that became a major part of how I learned. Radio was going through a DIY revolution. Because the recording technology got good enough for broadcast, there was an explosion in everyone's ability to produce radio. For me it meant walking around and talking to people and interviewing people about ideas. I started channeling my studies into radio pieces that I made. It was all of the things that I would have gone to grad school for: literature, philosophy, thinkers like Kierkegaard, Nietzsche, and Foucault who fascinated me. It was the same kinds of conversations my friends were having in their grad school classes. It was definitely my own curiosity that drove a lot of the work that I did in terms of reading and learning, but it was also the desire to share it. Having public output and public conversations about what I was reading and studying became part of the learning process. I also think that one of the reasons I'm attracted to this art is because it makes a record of what I'm learning and thinking about. The shows are the way I retain things. They're a journey of asking questions and getting answers and building upon what I've already done before.

Working in the media is a little bit of a cheat in terms of getting access to people. For example, one time I went to Copenhagen, where Kierkegaard lived and where his archives are. I've always had questions about his *Stages on Life's Way*. For years it's been a very important book to me. I did a very fun piece about

Kierkegaard for a Danish radio podcast that let me talk to all kinds of people. I went to the Kierkegaard Research Centre and I just wandered into conversations with Joakim Garff, who is one of the primary Kierkegaard scholars in the world. My show, *Too Much Information*, is all about mixing everything and everyone together, experts and nonexperts, and talking about ideas. The funny thing about the podcasting explosion is that a regular radio producer can't understand why an author would want to talk to a podcaster rather than being on National Public Radio. But if an author gets a nice respectable email from someone who is actually interested in what they wrote about, why in the hell would they not talk to a podcaster who wants to give them five minutes of airtime? It's the quality of the asking. It's all about having an interest in their knowledge.

I learn so much from interviewing people as my job, and it gives me a lot of feedback on what I've learned and that I understand these heady writers just as well as anybody else who studies them. I also had the perfect confirmation that my self-study was a big success when I met an upcoming young Nietzsche scholar who was a friend of a friend. When we hung out and talked, I realized that I had done just as well on my own and perhaps maybe even better. I didn't feel like I was not qualified to talk about some things because I wasn't in school. I have to say that I came away from that meeting feeling not only happy and pleased with the decisions that I had made, but feeling that maybe my decisions were even better than his, and that I understood as much of it as he did. Here was someone who did what I was thinking about doing but yet he and I were on the same level!

I think everybody should try this. Recently an intern of mine told me that she was thinking of applying to grad school. I told her that that was absolutely the stupidest thing that she could possibly do. Going to study literature or language or humanities or art or history and pay thousands and thousands of dollars is insane. I told her I learned more making podcasts than I did in school.

Benjamen Walker's website is wfmu.org/playlists/TI

Dorian Taylor

"Everything I've learned to satisfy some extrinsic goal has been faddish and empty by comparison."

Dorian Taylor *has been a designer, programmer, information architect, and now works as a consultant solving system-level problems for businesses. He left the public school system at 15, just after 10th grade, to attend an experimental, nonaccredited "un"-high school.*

Dorian gives a rich example of an associative learning process in action, and describes the advantages of that approach for the complexity of his thinking and his ultimate understanding of new areas of knowledge.

Learning is—literally—my job. Whether they know it or not, companies hire me to come in completely ignorant, and compose, from scratch, an understanding of whatever they're up to, which I communicate back to them. Everything else is a byproduct of that process. I've never had a problem finding work. When I was first starting out, it was a deterrent when I saw "must have bachelor's or master's in x." What's funny about that though is I found out that they don't actually care. From my perspective, and hearing about it from people who do hiring, most of the time they just say that to lessen their workload by scaring people off. It took me a while to clue into that. You can be pushy and just apply anyway. It's worked out for me.

I don't have a problem putting enormous effort into learning. I do have a problem with rote drills and sequences designed for administrative convenience. The conventional matriculation schedule is so tight that if anything knocks you off the rails on the way to university, you might as well not bother. And so it did. I burned out trying to earn impressive grades in spite of my disdain for the process. When that failed, I went to a place that to call it a school would insult it. There I had the license to learn whatever I wanted, and it was the "learning consultants'" job to connect me with real people in the real world who did the relevant work. Of course the organization wasn't accredited, which was the fatal torpedo to my already-foundering chance at a regularly-scheduled undergrad program.

At my present age of 33, I suspect I could get into any institution that would take my money. But I couldn't tell you why I'd go, other than for content I couldn't access outside such an environment, say for budget (e.g., particle physics) or regulatory purposes (e.g., law). The only thing that I do regret about the path I took is not experiencing the social aspect of what it's like to go to a university, or live in a dorm and get into the kind of trouble that only a high concentration of post-adolescents can. Keg stands, for example. In that way, I do feel a bit removed from the common experiences that other people share.

The way I approach new things is I start with what's interesting to me, which is invariably connected analogically to something I'm already familiar with. I find curricula to be like dictionaries: All too easily forgotten that the shape of a certain concept, or structure thereof, is a matter of its author's opinion, and not a natural law. Moreover, a curriculum tends to imply that a given body of knowledge is an ordered tree, when it's really a much more complex structure, one for which top and bottom—or first and last—are not meaningful concepts. We can waste a lot of effort looking for the right place to start in an uncharted body of knowledge, which is what curricula inadvertently teach us to do. And even the most expertly-designed curriculum can't tell you why we're learning (in that context, that's the job of an astute and compassionate teacher). In my experience, the single most important criterion for learning something is wanting to. Genuinely intrinsically so. Everything I've learned to satisfy some extrinsic goal has been faddish and empty by comparison.

I don't impose a structure on my process. I'm not sure how I could. If I had the information I needed to put the material in the most efficient order, I'd already know it all. Instead of thinking in terms of "top-down" or "bottom-up," I think in terms of "here to there" or indeed many "heres" to many other "theres." Structure emerges over time. It is essential, however, to encode my progress into copious artifacts—which can be anything from computer programs to Lego gizmos, but most often manifest as pencil on paper. The best materials are cheap enough that I don't hesitate to destroy them in the process of using them in some unexpected way. I have a four-drawer cabinet full of legal-sized manila folders full of what I call worksheets: Standard copier paper, turned landscape, dated, scribbled all over in mechanical pencil. This is how I do just about everything, or at least start. Com-puters are great, but only for well-defined, repetitive tasks. Their utility in the process of coming up with the structures they will later execute is limited.

Unless the steps to gaining comprehension are well understood, like learning a musical instrument, or sport, or a topic so heavily trafficked that an elementary textbook can be written about it, the process is literally—as in it exhibits an identical behavior to—a scavenger hunt. A first clue might send you to the other side of town, where you find a second clue that sends you to a third clue almost right back to where you came from. There is no way to optimize this process and pick up the two items close together before proceeding to the distant one, because you won't know the position of the third item until you reach the second.

A couple years ago, I caught up with an old friend who had since gotten an MBA and started a business, and we got on the subject of my learning (and inductively, professional) process. I told her it takes what it takes what it takes, and she couldn't accept the notion, citing investors, ROI, budgets, and deadlines. Solving problem X may indeed take arbitrarily long, but in the interim you will solve other problems which will be valuable—and even salable—in their own right. The idea is not to be so transfixed on X that you ignore serendipitous opportunities. It really is the only sane way to tackle any process that depends on the effective synthesis of disparate and eclectic material. Too much focus on a narrow objective, and too much emphasis on efficiency before achieving effectiveness, is guaranteed to make its acquisition take longer—every time.

Dorian Taylor's website is doriantaylor.com

Molly Danielsson

"We decided that in order to stick with our crazy plan we had to start telling people about it so they'd hold us to it."

Molly Danielsson and her boyfriend Mathew Lippincott started the Cloacina Project (named after the Roman goddess of the sewers) to create ecological sanitation systems that could support communities instead of draining their nutrients. They've become experts in the field from two years of intense study and developing connections to experts and enthusiasts. In that time they've legalized site-built composting toilets in the state of Oregon, demonstrated their portable composting toilet business at a festival of 500 people, and started teaching their approach to artists and designers at the graduate school for Collaborative Design at Pacific Northwest College of Art.

Molly started her business from scratch, and has reached expert status in ecological sanitation without formal education. Her process has included scholarly research, legal research and advocacy, and constant experimentation. All of this depends on her connection with a very supportive learning community, and her consistent work to share what she's learned in as many ways as possible. She's a great example of how making her goals public and feeling responsible to her community has kept her motivated.

Mat and I finished school, and we wanted to find a way to support ourselves by starting our own business. We decided to start recycling human waste through the most high-profit and most-loathed means possible, portable toilets. After crunching the numbers on portable toilets we determined that the most profitable aspect of the business is festivals and other short-term events. We had to learn everything about ecological sanitation, how composting toilets work, how to build them, how to maintain them, and how to navigate the legal issues surrounding them. When we started we didn't know any of this. The legal issues were hard. Mat read the rules, but we didn't directly approach the bureaucrats at first. I wish I could have called up the right regulator and just told them our full plans and gotten a real answer. That was too risky, so I called up claiming to be a student researcher asking hypothetical questions. Eventually we got an appointment to meet with the regulator who would oversee us. We got some real answers, but they just didn't know how to handle our case since we weren't mixing waste with water, which is what regular sanitation does, and that's what's regulated. Even in municipalities where the laws are clear, it's still a gray area. I ran into a group of incredible squatters in Switzerland who were running a portable composting toilet out of a squat mansion by a lake. They'd been running the business for three years even though it was technically illegal in Switzerland. Who's their most frequent client? The city of Geneva has hired them for the past two summers to run toilets and urinals outside the bars in the summer.

We wanted to get involved in advocacy to change the laws because it makes good sense environmentally, and it's in our interest. We have a good friend who works on public restroom advocacy, and she has lots of experience with regulators. She told us we needed to beef up our résumé—that would make our self-study seem impressive to regulators, since ultimately we're going to stay in Portland and we need the regulators who will oversee us to like us. We did two things that helped make all our independent learning seem more legitimate. We attended the required classes for certified septage haulers. We attended a two-month workshop in Switzerland for "young professionals" looking to start enterprises in water and sanitation. Nothing looks fancier on a résumé than a program in Switzerland, so we applied and got in. The program normally costs about $2,000, but I was able to work out a trade with the program by writing fact sheets for their online Sustainable Sanitation and Water Management toolbox. We felt totally isolated and cut off from our community while we were there, but it was worth it. It was that little thing that looked good on our résumé. We got a gig doing portable composting toilets at a local festival and were offered a teaching position at a local art school. Even the Centers for

Disease Control and Prevention called us about doing an art show on sanitation. We also benefited from the fact that the Gates Foundation decided to make ecological sanitation a major priority around that time.

After that, we got a grant from the Bullitt Foundation to encourage the Oregon Department of Environmental Quality to adopt performance-based codes. We got two major codes adopted in October 2011 that legalize site-built composting toilets. As part of the grant from the Bullitt Foundation, I've focused most of my energy this year on pushing for more regulatory changes through hosting lunch-and-learn events with regulators and the public, but it's really slow going. I've done a series of infographics and I'll be launching a short video explaining how sewers and septics work and other alternatives that exist.

Now, we've gotten enough rules changed so that we can finally start our portable composting toilet business to serve festivals. Over the next year we're going to be assembling a team to work with us on starting this business. The goal of launching the porta-potty business is to let people use them at festivals and experience a different toilet with their own bottom. We've done the legal legwork, we know the regulators now, and realize that our original idea of just starting a composting porta-potty business is the most direct form of education we can do.

That's where we've gotten and what we've done so far. When we first got started, we framed a research question: Is it possible to make a neighborhood sanitation system (toilets and graywater) that's low maintenance, affordable, and meets Western hygiene ideals? The question changed the more we got into the research. I wish we had rewritten the question on the wall at the beginning of each week to give us direction.

The first thing we did was move to the most composting-toilet-friendly legal setting in the country: Portland, Oregon. We spent our first month looking for advocates who could help us learn about the legal hurdles to our business plan. We found the most amazing group of grassroots anti-authoritarians working to legalize sustainability through a project called ReCode of Tryon Life Community Farm. Mathew spent the first winter in Oregon in libraries researching sanitation, wastewater treatment, and domestic septage law.

We decided that in order to stick with our crazy plan we had to start telling people about it so they'd hold us to it. I know I won't do good work unless I have someone watching me. So having a community is really necessary for that as well as for people to learn from. I need people to watch me and give me feedback at useful intervals. We worked hard to find our community. I met one person through a Research Club brunch. Research Club brings together a variety of people to talk about their passions over brunch. She was doing a homemade master's degree on ecological sanitation. She helped us host an awesome discussion about sewage, called "Talkin' Shit." We met several people through Transition Portland and DorkbotPDX who have given us feedback on our work and have come over for studio visits, and collaborated with us on certain aspects of projects.

We formed a salon with some friends who are also doing home DIY composting toilets. This has been one of the best things for our design process. The group meets to show our composting setups and give each other constructive advice on our composting process and issues we're having. Then we have a potluck. I contacted a friend who I knew had a composting toilet and he invited folks that he knew who were doing it and it grew from there. Now people hear about it and ask to join.

To help explain what we were up to, we decided to make educational posters about toilets, sewage, and composting. It was a great break from research for us to collaborate in a way that had a clear end goal. We had enough money to print the posters but we wanted to build our social credit in the community, so we asked three of our friends and mentors to lend us a total of $800 to print the posters. We had to pay them back from the sales. This was a great trick. It made us work our butts off to sell $850-worth of posters. It also showed us that people thought we were worth investing in. We were so honored that people had "invested" money in us that we started doing "investor updates" to tell them how our posters were selling, about talks we were giving, and to keep them abreast of our research.

Now they've become a board of mentors we look to for support and advice. I had one-on-one meetings with them to review our goals and got the feedback that we needed to start looking for outside funding, to start promoting our work, and to take more credit for our endeavors. We put a lot of energy into our presence online. Since we were among the few people in the US being really vocal about our enthusiasm for waste composting online, a lot of people started contacting us, so now we're even more connected with experts on this.

Even with our connections, I'm still not completely sure whose information to trust in the realm of sanitation. As far as toilet design, I only trust my nose. If the toilet doesn't smell, it works. The problem is it's impossible to tell from photos whether the toilet smells like rotten eggs. While we were in Switzerland, I found out a lot of the studies we had read about were seen as total failures. It confirmed our assumption that with bathroom design the most important thing is that users like the system and are willing to maintain it. Novel toilet systems cannot be forced on people. So, I only trust people who use the systems they make and advocate for.

Measuring our progress is easy. There are pretty clear indications of success and failure. We can monitor our compost piles to determine if they're performing. We can test our bathroom designs on strangers to see if they're acceptable. We've tested our knowledge of the legal and technical processes at the Oregon Water and Environment Short School for septage haulers and at the program in Switzerland. I was really surprised when we went to Switzerland to find out that I was on equal footing with the other students who had master's degrees in both environmental engineering and ecological sanitation. In those fields you don't get much experience in public speaking or writing. Since I have constantly had to describe what I've been doing for the past two years, I've gotten a lot of experience explaining this topic, and I think that's part of how we got where we are in terms of reputation.

We're experts on all this now, though I feel so uncomfortable being called an expert. We got there through intense reading, by sharing what we were learning, and by getting involved in communities of people who cared about the issue. I liked college, but learning independently has been a very different experience. Since I was moving at my pace and I was personally motivated to learn the material, I gained a real depth that I couldn't have achieved if I wasn't answering personal research questions. So we went from wanting to find a way to make a living doing something we cared about and knowing very little about it, to being respected experts in the field, without the degrees that most of the other experts have.

Molly Danielsson's website is <u>mdml.co</u>

FILM

Astra Taylor

"We all know how movies work. And we know when they don't work. So we know a lot. More than that, I think you learn much more by doing."

Astra Taylor *has made two feature-length documentaries about philosophy—*Zizek! *(2005) and* Examined Life *(2008)—as well as several short films. As a writer, she's contributed to* N+1, Monthly Review, Adbusters, London Review of Books, Salon, Alternet, *the* Baffler, *the* Nation, Bomb Magazine, *and other outlets. You can read about her ideas and experiences with informal non-school education in a Kindle Single called* Unschooling. *Recently, she has been involved with the Occupy movement, Strike Debt, and has written about it for* N+1 *and the book* Occupy!: Scenes from Occupied America *(2011). Until age 13, Astra did her learning at home with her three siblings, without a formal structure.*

Astra's motivation for writing and filmmaking is that both genres are the province of independent learning, and give her the structure of a long-term project to focus her self-education. She describes how she learned filmmaking on the fly. Having taken a job to make a short documentary, she convinced a more experienced friend to work with her, and treated the experience as an informal apprenticeship.

I'm a filmmaker and a writer, but neither of those is something I studied formally. Why would I choose those fields? Because they're actually ways of working that let you pick something to learn about and do it as part of a larger project. Being a filmmaker is an excuse to drill into a subject for two years and really learn about it. Or with writing, whether you're writing an essay or a book, you pick a subject and get to obsess over it.

I've made my name as a filmmaker, but really I always wanted to write. I shifted gears when I saw the movie *The Gleaners and I* by Agnes Varda. I was just astonished when I realized you can write with movies. It turns out that film is part of a genre called "essay film," but I had no concept of that. Seeing that movie was a pivotal moment. I discovered that there was another medium besides writing that lets you explore the world, combining words with pictures and sound.

I wanted to learn how to do it. So I basically scammed my way into filmmaking in 2001. There was a nongovernmental organization (NGO) in Senegal working to promote the nutritional use of a local tree called the Moringa tree. You can pick the leaves and dry them and make powder that is full of vitamins E and A and calcium. This amazing vitamin source is literally growing everywhere, but local people didn't know much about it. The NGO was looking for someone to make an instructional video showing you how to pick these leaves, how to dry them, how to use the powder, and to document the effects of the supplement for two months on infants who were severely malnourished. I said I would do it. The problem was I did not know how to shoot video and I did not know how to edit video. And I didn't speak French, which is one of the languages in West Africa. So I got my friend who had been to Senegal, spoke French, had gone to filmmaking camp in high school, and had access to a university's editing system. She ended up being my mentor for a few months. All I did was organize the field trip. By watching her, I learned the basics. Stuff like what's a cutaway, what B-roll is, and how to put a wireless microphone on someone.

She didn't know I was doing this. I never really said to her, "I'm siphoning off all your skills!" I think at the time I acted like I was carrying my equal weight. But I was really focused on observing everything she did and taking it all in. Why are you doing that? Why are you doing this? How are you doing it? I never felt ashamed that I didn't know, though I sometimes felt frustrated by my limitations. It's only in retrospect I see how much I learned from her. For example, audio fades. It never occurred to me that you could cross-fade audio tracks and that's why it works when scenes switch and it's not jarring to the viewer. Or, logging footage. When we came home the first night, she just started logging what we shot. I never would have known to do that. But these are the basic building blocks of how you make a film. Really I learned by attaching myself to this project and to her, so I am very grateful.

When I came back to New York, totally through luck, a friend of a friend was starting a documentary film production company. There was a little political documentary bubble that started right after 9/11 around when George W. Bush was first elected. I got a job wrangling people to be in a film about Muslim communities after 9/11. But I also got to watch experienced filmmakers work. What did I learn from them? I learned about the architecture of the film. They took a very formal approach. Instead of interviewing people in their homes, they brought people onto a set. When I first saw that, I thought that was unnatural and that it would be better to show people in their own homes. But then, when I watched the final edit, I realized it actually served the film. There was an aesthetic and formal consistency that made it much more powerful. So that was like my film theory. I don't actually read film theory and I don't even watch very many movies. I don't particularly like watching movies because I find them kind of emotionally exhausting, but maybe I also just like depressing ones. But really you don't need to know the history of cinema inside and out to make something valuable. We live in such a mediated environment that we all know how movies work. And we know when they don't work. So we know a lot. More than that, I think you learn much more by doing, i.e., by experimenting and making some mistakes along the way.

I guess in film school, you do learn basic technical skills. And some people are amazingly gifted in terms of their shooting ability or their editing or what postproduction they can do. It's nice to know what's possible in this realm, which of these are important skills you can learn in school. But I also could have studied them on my own if I was motivated. To a degree, I regret that I haven't cultivated those specific skills more. Instead I work with other people who have. My M.O. since that first trip to Africa is to find other people who know more than me and then pull them in, use their talent and technical skills, and glean what I can along the way, rather than learning those skills myself.

I don't shoot, maybe at some point I should so I can be more of a one-woman show. I think there would be an intimacy, when actually filming, that would be pretty powerful. Cinematography seems like a field people can definitely master on their own, once they have the gear. And with those technical skills, you'd have a way better chance at earning a living than I do. So I'd recommend it.

On the other hand, in my own case, I missed that boat. I don't have those skills so I can't really never work for someone else, and I'm not unhappy about that. I mean, a lot of people burn out. If you got into filmmaking because you really want to make your own films, because you want to make films you care deeply about, you also have to make a living. Then you're hiring yourself out and you risk draining your enthusiasm for the art form by working on other people's projects—things you don't believe in. When you're often working on things that you don't quite like, being a hired hand can make it hard to keep the necessary energy and enthusiasm to do your own projects. Your day job becomes something you kind of like and kind of don't. If you can't unite making your living with the thing you love, which is obviously ideal, then sometimes it's best to keep them totally separate. If I was working on other people's sets or in advertising or in features and narrative films that I didn't think were making the world a better place, I'm sure I would not want to make my own movies in my free time. The point is that, for me, filmmaking is really a vehicle, a way of exploring the wider world. You don't need to go to school for it; it can help make the world your school.

Astra Taylor's website is <u>hiddendriver.com</u>

Jim Munroe

"If you learn to do something when there are real stakes, you remember what you've learned more."

Jim Munroe *is a novelist and all-around indie culture maker who experiments constantly and shares both what he makes and what he learns about how to make it. In addition to novels, he's known for his post-Rapture graphic novels, lo-fi sci-fi feature movies, and award-winning text adventure video games. He also works occasionally for clients whose work inspires him.*

When I started researching this book, an acquaintance sent me a long list of people I should interview. Jim Munroe was at the top of the list. He's taught himself every medium he works in. In his early years learning to be a writer, being a part of the zine publishing community and putting his work out in the world gave him both feedback and motivation to continue. Later, he learned book publishing from the ground up to become a successful self-published writer. Jim tells the story of how he achieved artistic success and financial sustainability as an independent publisher, and explains the learning process he's gone through as he's become a filmmaker in recent years. Jim's experience supports the idea that learning by doing in a real-world context leads to richer, more thorough knowledge and skills.

Until I got to university, the schools that I went to were fairly conservative and didn't have things like creative writing classes, never mind anything arts related, not even a basic writing course. So school wasn't really catering to what I was interested in. But, you know, I think that if I had gone to a very artsy school, it could have killed me with kindness. Part of what I needed to do as a teenager was to be doing the exact thing they didn't want me to do in school. If writing had been legitimized, it would have taken some of the joy out of it for me.

When I was 17, I published my first zine and started to participate in the zine community. That meant getting my work out in front of an audience and getting feedback, even though it was obviously a very small print run. The process of writing something and getting it out in the world felt like a completed circle, as opposed to writing something that had to sit on your computer or sit in a desk drawer. That was really writing.

I published a short story collection and two novellas myself, and then I wrote a full-length novel. I wanted a publisher, so I got a book called *Be Your Own Literary Agent: The Ultimate Insider's Guide to Getting Published* by Martin P. Levin that explains the format that publishers are used to seeing, which is a cover letter, sample chapter, synopsis of the book, and a bio. I sent out 60 packages and got six responses. HarperCollins made an actual offer. I've been told again and again since then that that's a highly unusual circumstance, and that usually publishing houses don't look through slush piles of unsolicited manuscripts.

I was uncomfortable with the ownership of HarperCollins. Rupert Murdoch is a very right-wing, notoriously cutthroat kind of businessman. I decided with my second book I was going to publish independently, even though HarperCollins was interested in it. That was in 2000, and I've been publishing books independently in Canada myself and then most often finding a simpatico publisher in the US.

I definitely feel like having one book out with a traditional publisher gave me more credibility as a writer, especially from people in the industry, because this kind of self-publishing is thought of as "vanity press." I was very aware of that kind of bias in the industry and that was a big motivation for going independent. I wanted to fight that. It became a bit of a cause for me, being in that coveted position as a published author and going the other way to prove that people can choose to self-publish for reasons other than desperation and last resort. I knew from my experience making zines that there were people independently publishing who were just as talented, if not more talented, than people getting published traditionally. In my case, independent publishing turned out to be much more sustainable and much more suitable to my temperament.

I share everything I learned about how to publish independently. It's important to me to demystify the process as much as possible by putting information on the web—do it yourself articles and "how-to" articles from the perspective of someone who has published on their own and wants to share that information rather than keep it locked up.

When I need help myself, I would prefer to be pointed to information, not have someone walk me through it, because there's that sense of discovery and learning on my own and not being handheld through the whole process. I prize that kind of style of learning—the sense of discovery and learning on my own.

I've gotten involved in so many different mediums and it's the same learning process every time. I start, and then later, I realize, "Oh that's why they do it like that." I have to learn the hard way to internalize what I'm learning properly. Certain things are very standard practices in any industry. People are told how to do things first, and then they go do it. For me, I just start by doing it and then learn things retroactively. I gain a deeper understanding of the mechanics of why things are done the way they are. You have these happy accidents where you do something the wrong way, but your work ends up having a different style or flavor by happenstance because you haven't gone through the normal route of learning how to do it. There's something qualitatively different about the work, in the end, which I really like. It's great as long as you don't mind looking like an idiot sometimes, which I certainly don't mind.

Now I'm making films. Casting was one thing I learned the hard way. We really wanted to avoid the bloated machinery of moviemaking. It didn't occur to me to do a call for actors in an official way. I felt like that was procrastinating. I thought, come on, let's just get on with it.

In the process of making a film, I realized the value of working with trained actors. Let's say you choose an untrained actor because they look the part, and are willing to take some time off to be in your crazy movie. You do four takes, and what you'll end up with is one take that has background noise or something else that makes it unusable. Then, of the three that remain, there might be one where the actor gets the line right. In the others, the line might be delivered a little bit woodenly or the way it's said doesn't deliver the exposition the way you need it to. When you're editing you're looking for the one that works best, and you use it even though the light isn't really great or the sound isn't good.

If you have a trained actor, they'll get the line right each time. It will be delivered well and you'll have three usable shots. One may be a little angrier, one may be a little bit lighter in tone, and one may have the lighting in a certain way. What I discovered is that the power of talented actors is really seen when you get to the editing room, because it gives you so much more of a palette to work with. If you're building a kind of tension, then you can use the slightly angrier one. If it seems like something is missing from a scene, you can go back and use a different take. Editing is really impacted by your choice of actors, which someone could have told me in advance, but I wouldn't have really understood it without seeing it in action.

I had to learn this and other filmmaking issues myself by seeing the result of doing them wrong. I had to live through the fear of having fucked up the movie because of a technical oversight or because of one thing that wasn't done properly. If you learn to do something when there are real stakes, you remember what you've learned more.

The way I learn is an equivalent of taking a machine apart and putting it back together again just to see how it works. But by taking it apart, by deconstructing it, and fixing something, you find out so many things. I find that learning process itself to be fascinating. In our kind of culture, we have shorthand now for everything: That's just the way it's done. And it probably does make sense, but you have to dig for the logic. You also sometimes discover there isn't any logic to it. Those are satisfying moments, where you're vindicated with this way of learning, because you can say: This accepted method is total bullshit. It's a lot of work to deconstruct how things are done and why. But there's also a lot of pleasure to be had.

Jim Munroe's website is <u>nomediakings.com</u>

ARTS

Molly Crabapple

"Basically I looked at the world through a lens of asking: Is there art there? If there is, it should be my art."

Molly Crabapple *dropped out of art school and has been making a living as an artist for five years. She sells her work, is hired to paint murals on the walls of swanky restaurants, and started Dr. Sketchy's Anti-Art School, a periodic gathering of artists of all stripes who "draw glamorous underground performers in an atmosphere of boozy conviviality" and learn from one another, now in 150 cities. She has funded two large-scale art projects on Kickstarter with great success.*

Molly has taken a different road to learning as an artist, getting her work out in the world, and supporting herself with her art. Art school didn't offer her much in the way of artistic development, so she found ways to learn her craft on her own. She emphasizes that art school fails to teach the most important things to know as an artist—the practicalities of how to make a living at it. She learned that on her own through life experience, trial and error, and asking other artists how they do it. An avid reader and conversationalist, she also possesses a nuanced fluency with the history of ideas and literature that matches or exceeds any college graduate I've met.

I've been drawing since I was a little kid. My mom is an illustrator. I was a bad high school student. I went to a very bad college called FIT, but I dropped out of it after three-and-a-half years. I don't feel I learned anything from school that I couldn't have learned another way. Both in terms of artistic skills and the skills needed to make a living as an artist.

Before college, I went to Paris, because I was obsessed with the Lost Generation writers and artists. I was seeing this guy, and he bought me a really beautiful, expensive leather-bound sketchbook. I was really afraid of messing it up. So I started studying and being conscious of pen and ink. I spent every single day drawing and drawing and drawing everything that I saw around me. I filled maybe 300 pages of this sketchbook in a month.

I was also a constant reader. At home, I lived next to this thrift store that sold paperbacks for 10¢ apiece so I would go and buy massive stacks of paperback books on everything. Everything from trashy 1970s romance novels to Plato. When I went to Europe, I brought with me every single book that I didn't think I would read voluntarily, because I figured if I was on a bus ride, I would read them. So I read Plato and Dante's *Inferno*, and all types of literature. I got my education on the bus.

When I came back from Europe, I was 19 and I went to the art school I eventually dropped out of. I also started working professionally as an artist, which to me means that I was making money from my work. That's a big part of my education as an artist, and nobody teaches that in school. I was an illustrator then and I did every sort of thing that you could to make money with art. I put posters up in all the delis around Chelsea saying I'd draw people's pets for $25. I also put up posters saying I'd draw people's *Dungeons & Dragons* characters at Forbidden Planet, the comics and games store. I harassed the owner of a local coffee shop to let me draw his favorite jazz musicians. Basically I looked at the world through a lens of asking: Is there art there? If there is, it should be my art.

I also stalked all these established artists that I knew and I begged them to let me take them out to lunch so that I could talk to them. I asked them about their first jobs. I would ask them how they got art directors to be interested in them. Mainly just technical career things. I wrote to every single magazine and paper I could find, and mostly I was ignored. Deservedly so; I wasn't very good. One of my first jobs was drawing covers for *Screw* magazine, an infamous porn rag with a history of hiring infamous underground artists to do its covers. I got that from just picking up a copy of the magazine and writing a letter full of bombast to the editor. The bombast appealed to him. I got my biggest paying job around that time by answering a Craigslist ad to draw for *Playgirl*. I earned

$1,600. I was 20, and it felt like a fortune. Then I took that money and invested it into making postcards. I got a list of art directors and I started getting jobs from the *New York Times* based on the postcards. I just kept getting more and more jobs. It was very gradual. I never had a big break.

As I said, when I started I wasn't very good, and I trained myself. I practiced a lot. I got better materials. One of the truths in certain types of art fields is that if you're working with cheap materials, your work will just look really bad. I stopped living in an unlit room, with three other roommates, where I had to work hunched over in the dark on the carpet. I just drew a lot. I drew and I drew and I drew and I drew.

I tended to like art instruction books from the golden age of illustration. Sometimes it's helpful to copy masterpieces or artists you like; when you copy someone, and you're working in an easy-to-figure-out medium like ink, you really learn how to get everything. It's like reading a book aloud. I would also just try to draw from life.

Early on I started keeping my "taskmaster notebook" which I carry with me all the time. It's subdivided into things I wanted to do that year as a to-do list, and then just this huge section of everything I've ever read. I keep notes on things I want to try that I've seen; for example, I found André Breton's notebooks and he did this amazing thing where he was writing, but writing in circles on beautiful pale green paper in white ink. It was a visually striking effect, so I'd made a note to try that and experiment with it myself.

When I was 22, I started Dr. Sketchy's Anti-Art School, which has become a real phenomenon. It's a life drawing class with underground performers and models done in an irreverent and accepting environment. People buy tickets to go and the performers are well paid for their time.

It happened because I had been working as an artists' model to make ends meet. The artists would never speak to the models, and this got me really angry. Sometimes I was in life drawing class as an artist, but when I was there as a model, I was like a chair. It felt degrading. I thought there was a real opening for a life drawing class where it was about the model as a person, not just a model as body with muscles and flesh. I had been drawing posters for burlesque shows and I knew all these amazing performers with incredible style, so I got one of them to pose in a dive bar and invited people to come draw her. I didn't know it would blow up so big. It's all over the world, and I've gotten so many opportunities from it, speaking all over the world and recognition in the press for both Dr. Sketchy's and my own art. It also means I have a network of people in most major cities who can organize events around me and get me invited to events. That's a huge advantage.

The upshot is I don't know that there is anything you can learn in art school that you can't learn on your own. I really don't know any special secrets that you're supposed to know to get there. There is the idea that you get connected to the gallery system, but I went to a lousy blue-collar school. If you go to a rich people school, in any major, you will get a network of rich people. If you go to a poor people school, you won't get a network of anyone. I totally understand why people go to Ivy League schools, so that they'll meet the future power brokers of the world. I just never had the grades or the money for that, so it wasn't an option for me. I made my own way.

I network with people who are outside my field—journalists, writers, performers—and I look for every opportunity in the entire world where there is a blank wall and I can put my work on it. I do every possible application of visual art. I have had super open eyes and I've been opportunistic, and because of the internet, I can talk to anyone I think is interesting and approach them to hire me or to collaborate with me. I've been making six figures as an artist since I was 26, without being represented by a gallery.

Of course I would love it if a blue-chip gallery called me up and said we would love to represent you. But a normal gallery, I don't know if I would make as much money. They would have to be selling a lot of my work and for twice the prices I'm getting now for me to make the same amount of money, since they take half. I have a really awesome life making a lot of money and drawing exactly what I want to without that. I don't feel my career is lacking without a gallery. I also object to the idea that as you're increasingly successful, by selling more expensive work, you're making art for fewer and fewer people. That's not how it works in any other field, not for writers or musicians. Why should it be that way for artists?

Molly Crabapple's website is mollycrabapple.com

Ken Baumann

"*You cannot and will not experience more in the classroom than you will on a set.*"

For the past four years, self-taught actor **Ken Baumann** *has been a regular on an hour-long, single-camera television show called* The Secret Life of the American Teenager *on* ABC Family.

Ken completed his high school education, which he describes as largely self-directed, at a charter school for students involved in performing arts. He describes acting as a craft best learned on the job and in collaboration with others.

Neither of my parents went to college. They both just started working right out of high school and they learned in the field, so I had that example. I know that college is the dominant mode, but for the most part I don't buy it, especially with the performing arts. You cannot and will not experience more in the classroom than you will on a set. I think it's much better to learn from people who are working with you as opposed to paying for a class once a week.

I started acting really early. I did a lot of school plays, and then when I was about 11, I started to do community theater. Pretty soon after that I got really interested in becoming a professional actor. I talked to my parents about it. We did some research and figured out that the first step was getting an agent. The way that happened for me was that my parents took me to a model/actor talent search. I got my first agent that way, and through a chain of recommendations I got an LA agent. Talent searches aren't all on the level, so if you're a parent, and your kid wants to get into this, you definitely have to use your BS detector and make sure the search feels relatively professional. If you're an adult, mostly those things are just for money. I have friends who have done it the hard way. They found enough work on their own. They built—or fabricated—a résumé and then submitted it cold to agencies with a nice cover letter and a headshot. It's easier if you get a referral. You can ask someone you know, who is familiar with your work and is represented by an agency if they'll give you an introduction. So knowing people and earning their respect is important.

I started with modeling and commercials, and also acted in independent shorts done by film students. It was all about learning from experience and taking every opportunity. I left regular school and went to a charter school that allowed me to work independently on my studies and get done in two years. I had auditions five to eight times a week, running around town, so it would have been nearly impossible to have attended a regular school and not be behind or have to repeat a year or do summer school.

In terms of learning the craft of acting, the independent way to learn is by doing. It's by working and making mistakes, but making them with professionals who are better than you and who can help you get to where you need to be. Performance is a hard thing to figure out, but it's a thing you just have to do, more so than reading books about method acting. You have to perform until you feel really comfortable being something that you're not in front of strangers. When you're comfortable, then your performance gets more subtle and refined.

I think apprenticeship is the best way to learn acting. There is so much in film and television that you cannot learn in a class. It's an entire technical language that's being spoken on set. You have to do your job in a collaborative way with so many people and work under all sorts of conditions that never get recreated in a class. For film and television in particular, there is no better way to learn. Even if you're working on cheap productions like little student films or you and a couple of friends are shooting around with a camera and trying to make something that sort of resembles what you've grown up watching.

For example, my past four years on *Secret Life* have been amazing for me, especially in terms of learning the language of film and television. I'm surrounded by about 120 people, in addition to the writers, producers, and actors. They are doing a very technical job and for me to know how that works is a huge advantage as an actor. The best thing you can do is be curious about everybody's job. If you're lucky enough to be on a set where people are investing their time and money and are trying to make something good, being curious is how you learn, and it's also how you show respect—both of which are really important. Your curiosity will help you absorb information that will make you feel more comfortable on set. I've gotten to a point now with this crew that I work with where it's super shorthand. You can guess what they're going to require of you in rehearsal; to not get in someone's light or to not look down when you say your lines, which is all just as important as your performance.

The beautiful thing about film and TV is that you can do scenes again and again. You can do them multiple ways, and ask for input. You have the chance to try things directors or other actors suggest to you, even if they feel a little bit wrong or uncomfortable, because you can just do it again.

Once you have some experience—for example, in community theater or local commercials or short films—and you want to work in film and television, the place to do it is in Los Angeles. There are a lot of alternatives, like New York, but for the most part, the big stuff happens in Los Angeles. If you want to get into it, find a way to move and live in the city in which you want to work. It's a hard thing to do, but get up the gumption and come to Los Angeles because it's the best place to do it.

Ken Baumann's website is kenbaumann.com

David Hirmes

"I just decided to experiment and iterate instead of going through some sort of formal, accepted training process."

David Hirmes *is a programmer, bookmaker, and photographer, among other obsessive pursuits, without formal training in any of these fields. He graduated from Hampshire College, a nontraditional college structured around self-directed learning.*

David instructively describes the happy medium between traditional classroom learning and the self-directed approach of Hampshire. He offers a great example of a project-oriented learning strategy. He gets interested in a technology, an idea, or a subject area and creates a project for himself that organizes his learning. Here he describes a project combining his interest in macrophotography and the opportunity for no-cost experimentation offered by digital photography.

As a kid, I was always curious and interested in all sorts of subjects, but I didn't particularly like school very much. During the summers I would read all of these books, like on history and math. I would expect that school would start in the fall and then these ideas I'd been reading about would get fleshed out in a wonderful way, in which I would understand them even more, and have that understanding lead me to ever more interesting places. Instead, I would get to school and it would be tedious. The teachers were uninspiring. Topics like physics, which were inherently fascinating to me, would be made completely boring. I mean, I think it actually takes effort to make a subject like physics dull. I just wanted to get to the real stuff so that I could do something with it or increase my understanding about the world.

For college, most of the places I looked at were alternative no-grade type schools, which for me combines what's good about school and what's good about independent learning. I took to Hampshire pretty well partially because it rewards the curious. Hampshire has few requirements and no grades. You do a ton of writing and you're allowed to take classes in a bunch of different areas of study. It was a beneficial way to approach learning for me, although I have vague regrets about not being forced to take certain classes because of gaps I find in my knowledge now. I used to joke that I probably should have gone to St. John's College, where they learn the classical canon in the original Greek and Latin—but I wouldn't have known that unless I had actually graduated from Hampshire.

Now I tend to organize learning something new around specific projects. One thing that's a really hard truth about real learning—whether it's in school or on your own—is every project that I'm really proud of and has ended up turning out really well has taken 10 times as much time as I thought it would. A good example of that process is, a few years ago, I got obsessed with photographing ice. It's macrophotography; very close-up shots of ice all taken in very controlled environments. They're shot in a way that a lot of times you don't actually know what it is at first. They look dynamic, like maybe there's some sort of action, frozen. They're all pretty small pieces of ice, with little gas bubbles that get trapped in the freezing process. That's what gives them the dynamic look. I would freeze water in bowls or balloons or other things of that size and take them out and often just light them with a flashlight or on plates in a totally dark room.

This was enabled by the availability of digital cameras. I got one pretty early and the idea of having an unlimited number of shots that you could take for free was still pretty new, so I was just taking pictures all the time and I never really considered myself a photographer. The great thing about the digital camera was that it was a technology that fit perfectly with my way of learning, which is a lot of experimentation. Unlike traditional photography, there was no penalty for trying something a thousand times. I didn't have to waste a thousand negatives and a thousand prints to try a thousand things. I could just keep shooting and never run out of film. It was a lucky confluence between this technology and my existing proclivity.

I've always been obsessed with macro/micro ideas: very large things and very small things. As I pursued this through digital photography, I did some reading and got kind of discouraged because the proper photographic equipment was really expensive and the techniques are really difficult and there are a lot of things to learn. The facts on the ground turned out to be a little different, because I was actually already doing stuff that I shouldn't have been able to do through this jury-rigged, accidental method that I figured out. I got a jeweler's lens and I just put the camera on top of the lens and the lens on top of something and realized that I could simulate a super expensive macro lens for nothing if I stood still enough and had the lighting right. And I realized that was working just as well as a whole professional setup. As often is the case with me, I just decided to experiment and iterate instead of going through some sort of formal, accepted training process. It often takes longer, but there's more of a chance I'll get to some unexpected place.

The process was that I would go to the kitchen every morning and I would open up the cupboards and I would look for interesting vessels to pour water into to freeze them and just completely fill the freezer with as many of these things as possible. I'd go off to work, come home, and then after everybody had gone to bed, take all those frozen shapes out, put them in the living room, which was totally dark, and just start shooting in as many ways as I could. I would take like 200 or 300 shots, upload them to the computer, and look to see what was interesting and what wasn't. For the things that were interesting, I would note the type of vessels and think about pouring salt on it or using this magnifying lens with this flashlight and then just head in the direction that looked promising.

I spent a couple of months doing this. I put the photos online and a lot of people just saw them. A gallery in Florida decided to put on a show. Then there was an article in the *New York Times* about photoblogs that featured my work. A huge blown-up version of one of my shots was on the cover of the Sunday Arts and Leisure section, and from that I got a bunch of shots put in *Seed* magazine and then in a book about ice. I haven't really done any photography projects since then. I never really identified myself as a photographer and I think people made that mistake, expecting more. That just happened to be a particular confluence of interests. It's funny. Talking about all this, I realize I have the capacity for learning a lot of stuff independently, so it makes me think about that classical St. John's College education I wanted. Even five years ago I would have said, "I'm totally going to go through the canon. It's on my to-do list." Now, turning 40 and realizing that time is in fact limited, I think it's more interesting to follow my actual interests than to go back and try to get some sort of completist notion of what an education or well-rounded person is. Back in college, I thought of all that as foundational rather than an end point. But I've already got a foundation. It's just some hodgepodge thing from Hampshire and 20 years of continuing to be a curious person, but it works for me. As much as I wanted to be like Indiana Jones who could be an adventurer and also knew his history and Latin, I'll probably just have to enjoy the movie, and actually spend my time making stuff.

David Hirmes' website is hirmes.com

Christopher Bathgate

"*Getting stuck for me has been one of my best teachers. It has taught me the huge difference between just knowing the answer, and knowing how to find the answer.*"

 **Christopher Bathgate** *is a self-taught machinist sculptor. He is a two-time recipient of a prestigious Pollock-Krasner Award and has also been awarded the Creative Baltimore Grant. His work is in numerous private collections across the United States and abroad. His sculptures have been exhibited in galleries in New York City; Brooklyn; San Diego; Cincinnati; Washington, DC; Maryland; North Carolina; and at the Baltimore Museum of Art.*

Christopher found that art school wasn't teaching him what he needed to make the art he wanted to make. Disillusioned with the curriculum and facing financial hardship, Christopher chose a different path to becoming an artist. He learned skills and made art simultaneously, learning what he needed to realize his ideas, and developing ideas to learn how to use specific tools and techniques. This project-based approach is a common one for independent learners, giving them a context and a need for what they're learning. Christopher's experience is an important testimony to an artist's ability to be successful without an art education or MFA. Like Molly Crabapple, he emphasizes that selling your work outside the gallery system is remunerative and doesn't limit public respect for your work.

I was always curious about how things worked and how things are made. Every object whose construction was not obvious fascinated me. I wanted to know how cars worked or how a toaster worked, and I often took things apart. I wanted to explore materials, mechanics, and everything in between. In hindsight, I probably should have been an engineer, but I am a hopeless creative type. Having spent my teenage years at an arts-oriented public high school, I decided sculpture was my calling. Most of my earliest attempts at sculpture quickly fell apart and were very poorly built. Because of that, I was very discouraged. But over time, I began to realize that what I was really lacking were the technical skills to properly execute my ideas.

So after high school, I went to a fine arts college seeking the skills I felt I lacked. At my school, we talked a lot about visual concepts and art theory, which are important. But we rarely, if ever, discussed practical knowledge, such as how to build things that wouldn't fall apart. We weren't taught carpentry skills, how to use power tools, how to utilize materials for their strengths, or about fasteners, glues, welding, and the rest of it. I found myself full of ideas that I could not execute for lack of information on how best to build them. I wasn't learning basic construction methods, and I felt that my lack of technical knowledge and skills, not art theory, was the greatest barrier to making my art, and they are the things I ultimately decided to teach myself.

I worked three jobs just to afford school, and at some point, I reasoned that if I was going to work this hard while going into debt, why shouldn't I spend that energy and money building a studio while gathering the equipment and technical knowledge I needed for a lifetime of making art? I had initially envisioned myself a few years down the road graduating art school with a BFA, a ton of debt, no tools or equipment, and few job prospects. The first day of my second year of college, I was disillusioned and broke. That morning on the way to my first class I finally decided to drop out. And while unsure of my choice, I walked right past the school, and never looked back.

Certain types of education are not necessarily worth the cost because either they embody inherently unteachable concepts, or they concern topics that are so straightforward that you can easily learn them on your own if motivated. For me, art is a good example of both such arguments. No one can actually teach you how to be creative; teachers can only expose you to basic skills for exercising creativity, and then sort of teach around it. This is helpful to some, but I found it lacking focus. I took on a little debt trying out school, saw that it wasn't for me, and then decided to try and make it on my own both out of necessity and frustration with my experience. Because of that choice, my artwork has flourished.

So, how did I do it? Mostly I learned by reading books, trial and error, and talking to other people with experience. I took a year off from making art after I dropped out and learned how to fix cars. That gave me confidence in my ability to tackle things on my own. If I could learn how to rebuild an engine all by myself, why couldn't I learn how to do other things on my own? I bought a welding torch and a grinder and set up a studio in an old rusty shed in my backyard. I started to teach myself how to be a sculptor in what I thought was a more logical way than the methods I had observed in school.

My approach was methodical and focused heavily on technique. I was drawn to metal work, so I started simply. I set about mastering one tool at a time. First, I learned basic torch work, which I had some exposure to in high school. Next, I picked up an electric welder, then a drill press, and on it went, one tool at a time. Eventually, I found myself doing complex machine work and dabbling in drafting, electronics, chemistry, and even robotics. Later on I designed and built my own computer-operated machine tools with the knowledge I had gained through my efforts.

Rather than doing practice exercises, I preferred learning while making my sculptures. I designed the pieces around what I was trying to learn. For example, I wanted to know the best way to turn a perfect sphere. First, I researched techniques and built the tools for that particular operation. Then I designed a spherical sculpture and worked on it until I learned how best to achieve the desired result. If I wanted to learn a different technique, such as thread cutting, I designed work to that requirement.

I always felt better learning and creating at the same time. It gave the work purpose, other than just being an artifact of my imagination, because I was also acquiring valuable skills. Working this way is what shaped the aesthetic I have today and continues to influence my work as I continue to learn new things through my sculpture.

One frequent problem of going it alone is getting stuck on a problem, as you usually have no one to guide you. When I was building one of my computer-operated machines, the controller just would not work correctly and I didn't know anyone who could help. I frequently used a few online forums I had found where people could point me in the right direction. There were also times when my research came up empty, and I was on my own. I would think for days about the problem and all its different parts. I would come up with a few possible solutions and try them; if they didn't work, it was back to the drawing board. Eventually, I would have a breakthrough and I would solve the problem. Doing things this way, I found that not only would I eventually find the answer, but also my understanding of the problem was so much more comprehensive and detailed than if I'd simply had someone else just solve it for me. Getting stuck for me has been one of my best teachers. It has taught me the huge difference between just knowing the answer, and knowing how to find the answer.

I did miss out on some opportunities and ways of being recognized early on in my career by dropping out of art school. Well, sort of. At my former college, the graduates were each given a senior exhibition at a small local gallery. I had a friend from school that I'd kept in touch with and we knew each other's work well. He was planning his senior show, and we talked about what a strange and mixed validation it was to be handed an art show simply because one had paid a lot of money to earn a degree. Regardless of the merits of the work, everyone got a show. My friend thought my self-guided work was as good as any of his fellow graduates. Being young and rebellious, he proposed a little scheme to help me share in some of the recognition he was getting. The day he installed his exhibition, we slipped six or seven rather large and unwieldy steel sculptures of mine into the gallery and displayed them alongside his. We never asked for permission. We just walked in, acted like we knew what we were doing, and pretended everything was as it should be and nobody questioned us. When the show opened a few hours later, everyone was delighted to see some very interesting work they had not expected to see. Even the faculty, who were understandably angry, begrudgingly admitted that the work was "not bad." They demanded my friend reveal my identity, but he refused. I stood there a few feet away listening to the heated exchanges, safe in my anonymity. The show was a hit and I had received my first taste of positive feedback from my peers. It was a valuable experience that helped spark my pursuit of more public venues and the desire to exhibit my work to a wider audience.

Today, my work is in a number of different galleries and I make my living as a full-time artist. Showing work at every available opportunity has proven to be the most useful strategy for me. Over time, one serendipitous event has led to another, and somehow managed to snowball into what now resembles a professional art career.

But true to my do-it-yourself spirit, I have never relied solely on art galleries to make my living or sell my work. I've cultivated my own private list of collectors over the years by networking and meeting as many people as I can. I've done everything I can think of to get exposure for my work, including writing to blogs, and magazines, and showing work at unconventional exhibitions in unusual locations. I have even gone as far as sticking a webcam on my machines while they work, just to see who will watch. With the help of a friend, I set up my own website, published my own art book, and have taken extra efforts to present my work to as wide an audience as possible. Art galleries still have a place because they are a meaningful venue and, in some way, still offer a form of validation for artwork. But galleries only have so many resources to give to a single artist, so they are only a piece of a larger strategy for artistic success. My modest accomplishments reinforce for me that doing it yourself is truly the best way to ensure something is done for your own greatest benefit. Because of that, I am doing what I love every day. And I can be proud of what I have achieved on my own, which is very satisfying.

Christopher Bathgate's website is *chrisbathgate.com*

ENTREPRENEURSHIP

Caterina Rindi

"I realized that, mainly, I wanted to run a business. If I didn't have the proper credentials, I wasn't going to let that stop me."

 **Caterina Rindi** *got her first job as a bilingual public school teacher without a teaching credential, and has worked in nonprofits and startups. In 2010, after she applied and wasn't accepted into an MBA program, Rindi started a small business and participated in creating alternative systems for educating herself and her friends.*

Caterina's story shows a person who wanted to advance her career and thought grad school was the answer. When she wasn't accepted to graduate school in her field, she changed gears and started a business instead. By reading and participating in learning communities she learned everything she needed to build the business without spending a dime on school. MBA grads usually leave school with a solid professional network, which is one of the frequently cited benefits of these programs. Caterina gathered like-minded friends and acquaintances to formalize an alternative network.

I wanted a graduate degree because I was frustrated professionally and wanted to move up a level. I had been doing a lot of program management for nonprofits, but I really wanted to move up to director level and I wanted to run my own nonprofit. I had applied for lots and lots of jobs, but nobody was interested in hiring me with just program management experience and so I thought that at least a master's or PhD in either business or education policy would kick me up to a level in which I would be considered for director positions. So, I applied to graduate school. But I didn't get in.

After that, I was really disillusioned with formal education. I realized that, mainly, I wanted to run a business. If I didn't have the proper credentials, I wasn't going to let that stop me. So I just started this little food business and it worked. San Francisco is full of trees in people's backyards that are just neglected. So I started "mo foods" to take this surplus food and turn it into preserves and pickles and things. I sold them at an underground farmers' market. The business had a great model to it because it was an exchange with the fruit tree owners. I gave some of the finished products to the people whose trees I picked from. They were so grateful to have me come pick their fruit so it wouldn't go to waste.

To figure out how to actually run the business, I read tons of business books and I thought about all of the different things that an MBA program should theoretically give me. I figured out how to achieve those without actually going through a program. A handful of my friends do have MBAs, so they are my informal advisors. When I had questions or I couldn't figure something out, I definitely had a lot of resources for that.

I also built some real infrastructure for collaborative learning. Right when I was starting the business, in 2010, a lot of my friends were looking for work and I was having lunch with various people to talk about the frustrations of looking for work. We talked about staying positive and taking care of ourselves. We also talked about networking and how our skills in one industry could transfer to another. I didn't have a steady income and within my social group there were also about 10 other people who were struggling in similar ways.

I emailed all of them and said, "Hey, how would you like to form a group and use that to help launch each other and increase our reach to other people who are looking for jobs?" They all said yes. So I started the Goldfish Networking Group. It was in my living room and I've been doing it ever since. The group emails each other to share opportunities and resources. We have about 30 people in the group right now. Last week I had two new members come in. We don't meet every single week if there aren't enough people who can come. I feel like we need at least five people to attend for it to be useful. We meet probably three times a month. It's a great model that I'd suggest for anyone looking to learn from and help support others.

I have success stories from that group of people who have started their own businesses. One member is an entrepreneur who went to Chile and got funded by the Chilean government to create another Silicon Valley there. Another owns his own dental office here in San Francisco. My brother joined the group and he is now working as a film editor for a nonprofit here in the city.

The other really key thing I did to substitute for what I'd get from an MBA was joining the Faux MBA reading group started by my friends Greg Veen and Samantha Gottlieb. It was 9 or 10 of my friends who also were interested in starting their own businesses or in understanding more about the way their employers made decisions and set directions.

It's been a great space to process a lot of the stuff that I'm reading. As a business owner I ended up really being isolated, and that's something that both the networking group and the book club have helped with. I can read all these business books, but the processing and synthesizing of that material is difficult to do myself. I can write and think about it and put some blog posts up, but the group discussions are really great opportunities to do that.

The curriculum is a group effort. Each of us had already chosen a few books that we found in different places, from online courses and from things we'd heard of. We started out with business theory and we read the original standby books that were 10, 15, 20 years old. They were incredibly dry. They were all written by white men.

We all said that we needed to get something that was more relevant to us. The next business book was *Financial Intelligence for Entrepreneurs* by Karen Berman and Joe Knight. It's a great book, incredibly practical. In contrast to the older business theory books, she breaks down a lot of the terms around financial management, defines really simple terms, and teaches you how to read an income statement and all the different kinds of people that you need when you have your own business.

We've gone around with theory, and with practical knowledge, and then things like Tony Hsieh's book *Delivering Happiness*, on the culture of Zappos, because that's really more modern. That's what's going on today. It's not something that anybody was talking about 30 years ago.

Something we did recently that was a great experience was we used a workbook called *Business Model Generation* by Alexander Osterwalder and Yves Pigneur. I was ready for the next step in my food business, which has evolved into Share | Kitchen, a food business incubator in San Francisco. For the book club, I sent them all my business plan, which was under construction, and we all worked on taking my business plan apart and putting it into this framework that the *Business Model Generation* workbook talks about. It was an amazing exercise. I couldn't have done it by myself; to have other people's eyes and perspectives on it was just great, totally valuable, and generous of them. We thought, well, yeah we could use it to figure out eBay's model, or we could figure out yours, so let's do yours. Things like this, learning about flexibility and personalization, make me think, it's possible that I have actually benefited by not going through a traditional MBA program.

The Faux MBA reading group's curriculum can be found on p. 184 in the **Resources** *section that follows these interviews.*

Find Caterina Rindi at *twitter.com/caterinarindi*

Jeremy Cohen

"Other entrepreneurs are basically my business school."

Jeremy Cohen *runs ExchangeMyPhone, a bootstrapped business that pays people for their old phones, or recycles them for free if they have no resale or salvage value. The company was founded in 2010, was paying its expenses two months after launch, and started hiring within four months. With his fiancée, Katherine Preston, Cohen now manages a team of eight. He's never been to business school and had no connections to the startup world when he founded his company.*

For the past two years I've run ExchangeMyPhone. We are making cell phone recycling as easy as returning a Netflix DVD. We have immense competition. Our largest competitor just received $22 million in funding. But really, I like to say that our biggest competition is drawers and closets. That's where 90% of used cell phones end up. I don't have any formal training in business, so we're also still learning on the fly and making mistakes and laughing at ourselves as we grow.

What we're doing is a little different than anyone else. Unlike any other buyback service we offer our customers the chance to donate the payout from their phone to any of the 765,000 US-registered nonprofits. We also offer same day payment, prepaid shipping for every cell phone in our catalog, and free recycling on all phones. Our customer service promises are central to who we are and we believe that doing good is good advertising in itself. Our biggest challenge is letting people know that we exist. Everything we do to accomplish this is stuff I had to learn from scratch.

I've taken a zigzag path to get here. Something that has always been a big part of my life is my stutter. Growing up I was not able to speak normally, or make the first impressions that I wanted to because of my speech. I have experienced failure just trying to say my name. These days, I'm no longer afraid of it and that courage has gotten me where I am.

I went to college in Walla Walla, Washington, and supported myself through school and beyond, by working a union job in Chicago as a beer man at sporting events and concerts. After graduating college in 2005 I did a lot of traveling and invested my time and money in real estate. I dabbled in starting a number of businesses but none of them truly excited me. I looked into the possibility of business school. I played with it for six months and decided that it was more formal and more structured than I wanted. I had been saving for years and I knew that if I were to put thousands of dollars of my own money into something, I wanted to start my own business. That way I would learn many of the same lessons without the incredible debt that business school can cause. I guess the biggest draw of business school is the networking, but I decided to save my money and use it to experiment in the real world.

ExchangeMyPhone builds on experience I already had. In many ways it's a continuation of my family business. My dad has run a used bookstore for longer than I've been alive. After dealing with used books my whole life, the phone recycling business fit very naturally. Besides that experience, one of the other things that allowed me to start ExchangeMyPhone is perhaps a delusional belief that I can do anything. And one of the things that has kept us in business has been learning to embrace that the people we work with are often better at what they do, and that I should take a step back.

In building the first version of ExchangeMyPhone, I had a hard time figuring out how to break into the industry. I did not take advantage of the resources in Chicago. I didn't know that the startup world existed, so I approached everything as though I was reinventing the wheel. I did not even attend Meetup groups or read startup-related blogs, though I could have easily increased my learning in that way.

For me, one of the awesome things about moving the business to New York has been getting more involved in the startup world and seeing what other people are doing, and learning from them. Other entrepreneurs are basically my business school. I follow business and startup blogs and newsfeeds, and learn a lot that way. And, having so many bright, successful, ambitious people to learn from and bounce ideas around with here in New York is priceless. In my case, finding all those people probably started with the Skillshare classes I took and grew from there.

I tend to do first, then ask questions and learn from my mistakes. I'm okay making mistakes and picking up the pieces even when that's unpleasant. I made a lot of mistakes in time as well as money. I don't think that the way I did things was the most efficient way, or the way that I would do them again. There was very much a sophistication curve but learning and improving as I go has allowed me to get where I am today. It has given me a sense that I can make anything work.

Generally, in running a startup, there is nothing that's too difficult and there's nothing that can't be learned. But there is a lot to be done. The biggest challenge that I have faced is the breadth of things to learn and manage. Everything from the specifics of web development to branding, user experience and design, web hosting, inventory flow, cash flow, accounting, tax implications and regulatory compliance, hiring, community building, marketplace tracking, customer service and communication, business development, marketing, networking, and—finally—ensuring that everybody still has a job next month.

When I need to learn about something I do a lot of reading and then I find someone who knows more about it than I do and take them out for coffee or lunch. In asking for their knowledge, people are even more willing and even more generous if you have done something to show that you're interested and you've made a commitment on your end as well. I never realized, or embraced, how valuable networking can be until I moved to New York. Leaving the comfort of my home in Chicago, and pushing myself to succeed in a new city, changed my outlook and shaped the direction of ExchangeMyPhone. Without that change and forced motivation, I don't think that the business would be where it is.

Jeremy Cohen's business is exchangemyphone.com

Simone Davalos

"It's just seeing where your resources are and building on your community and then it's equally important to give back."

 **Simone Davalos** *is Owner of ComBots LLC. Her work cen-*
ters on robotics education and the promotion of tomorrow's
engineers. ComBots LLC seeks to provide an entertaining and
educational experience in robotics and engineering for audi-
ences of all ages. Their exhibitions—the ComBots Cup and
RoboGames—as well as private corporate events, combine
the excitement of extreme sports events with the solid foun-
dation of engineering and art. She is a college graduate and a combat robotics referee.

As Simone told me, you don't get to be a combat robotics referee by going to
school. She describes the joyful process by which she's learned the technical—and
pyrotechnical—skills she uses in her robotics work, as well as the immersive learning
process she has gone through to put on the combat robotics competitions she and her
husband produce. Simone is a great example of the value of communities in learning
and in making things happen. It's a simple rule: You ask for help, and you give back
when others ask you.

I have absolutely no engineering background except for what I taught myself. I just was always into that kind of thing. I was always into building and I was always into taking stuff apart. I think the highest compliment I ever got was from my father. He turned to me at one of my events and said, "You know, you were always a weird little kid." I have always had a thing for engineering anything that goes "boom!"

I got a degree in English at Yale. I learned some things in classes. I can put a sentence together and I can read, but what I learned that was useful to how I make my living now came from outside of any sort of academics. Mainly, I learned how to blow stuff up, which happened in the marching band. I'm not musical at all. I like to hum occasionally. But it wasn't only for musicians. At my school, all the clubs court the freshmen. They do all the songs and dances like, "Join our club," "Join our secret society," "Do our things." It wasn't really me, and I didn't know what to do. Then all of a sudden this huge, enormous crowd of incredibly loud, crazy people were running screaming down the aisles. And they started playing the fight song really loud and throwing tee shirts into the audience and saying, "You don't have to be a musician, you don't have to know how to sing, you don't have to do anything but come join our band and it will be fun." I thought, I could use some fun. I like fun.

So I showed up to the meeting and they said, "Hey, great, here, hold this duct tape, we're making a life-size locomotive out of plywood and duct tape and a fire extinguisher. We want to see if we can get the lights to work on it." That's what I did for four years. I figured stuff out largely through osmosis. When you joined the band, you had to figure out what you were doing. You pretty much just learned from the people that went ahead of you. So the seniors were invaluable because they would pass along this knowledge. It was both an oral tradition and a written tradition. We had a book of stuff that had been written down since around 1980. It was this giant composition book that was stuffed with examples of things and plans and sketches and notes and "Don't do this. We did this one time and just trust me, you don't want to do it that way."

Now I run RoboGames with my husband. RoboGames is the world's largest open robot competition. It's like the Olympics for robots and we have about 60 different events. We get about 1,000 roboticists to come from all over the world to participate. This is our 10th year doing it and it involves a lot of logistics and equipment and mechanical engineering and delegation and a lot of event promotion and event logistics. I got started in that 10 years ago. I met my husband and he put on robot events. So I got involved. I learned about sumo robots and I learned about competitions and I learned about international Japanese robot happenings. It just cascaded and our events got bigger and bigger until finally we were working for the show *BattleBots* on Comedy Central.

When *BattleBots* finally shut down, David turned to me and said, "Hey, we should keep doing this. All we do is we put on this event and we sit around and watch robots fight all day, all the time!" So we bought the arena and we quickly realized there was more to it than we thought. It was a lot of learning on the job and baptism by fire. Literally. We were just a mom-and-pop operation so I had moments like, "I guess I'm going to have to learn how to drive a forklift because that truck ain't going to unload itself." I can now operate a forklift elegantly. I give elegance to operating a forklift.

We have professionals in all the places that we need professionals now. For example, we have a professional materials guy who comes in if something breaks on the arena and needs to be fixed the right way rather than "okay, let's patch it back together and hope nothing bad happens." We have a really crack arena crew that's been doing it for easily seven or eight years and we have new people all the time who get that received wisdom. Again, there's no place you can learn how to do it, you just have to do it. It's an iteration. You can't learn how to do it anywhere. You can't take classes. You can learn how to use the machines that will eventually build your robot and you can consult with other people who have built robots in the past, but really the only way to learn how to do it is to actually do it, and this is from the event operation side as well as the robot building side. There are a lot of people who did a lot of things that you can't learn in school.

Finding people to work with isn't universally easy. I'm in a very lucky position because we're in the San Francisco Bay Area where combat robots and art robots and that sort of thing kind of took hold at a very early stage. You have this whole underground art scene and you work off the community, which I figured out is the best way to get in contact with people and make things happen. Let's say you wanted to put on a show, and it's something no club is going to let you do.

But, hey I know, let's do it in the junkyard! Because I was down there the other day and they were talking about all the art that people were making there. But to do that, you had to know a guy. Someone who knows another guy, who knows a girl who does the same kind of thing, and suddenly you have this community that you've tapped into. Every time we did a show at a new venue, we'd keep all the contact information and we'd talk to all the people who had done shows at that venue before, and we'd end up with a really good informational resource to go back to. Before iPhones and BlackBerrys, I had a folded piece of paper in my pocket at all times, in case we needed somebody to come and do acoustical stuff because the neighbors were complaining. I'd look at the list and see that a certain person used to do sound engineering for big concerts. He might know someone who can do that. It's just seeing where your resources are and building on your community and then it's equally important to give back. When someone helps us out, if they need a door person to work three nights for their show on surrealistic Dada performance art happenings, I'll do that. So that's essentially what we do with robotics.

I'm not sure we'd be able to do this if we were not in a place that had this sort of entrenched artsy community; it would be harder to do. It would be possible, but it would be really hard. But not impossible. A few years ago, there was an Eagle Scout who was really interested and curious and ended up collecting smoke detectors and building a reactor out of them, in his backyard. He just did it because it was fun, because he thought it was interesting. He got in huge amounts of trouble for it. But, now of course people are going to offer him jobs all over the place because they have seen that he is a really intelligent kid who's got the capacity to find it in himself to do something where he wasn't surrounded by people who were already doing it.

Simone Davalos' business is <u>RoboGames.net</u>

TECHNOLOGY

Harper Reed

"*I try to surround myself with incredibly smart people who are often, if not always, smarter than me. Because other people are so important to learning.*"

Harper Reed *served as the Chief Technology Officer for Obama for America during the 2012 election; before that, he was* CTO *at Threadless. He is an engineer who builds paradigm-shifting technology and leads others to do the same. He loves using the enormity of the internet to bring people together.*

Harper is a wonderful example of a person who loved the experience of school, but found that the most significant learning he has done comes from his independent education. He emphasizes the importance of learning new things in a real-life context, and the experiential, project-oriented process by which he usually learns. His advice about how to contact experts for help is invaluable.

I love computers and I've always been around computers. I can't really talk about education without talking about computers. I went to high school and I actually really loved it. I took all the classes I could, I was prom king, student council president. I did everything I could to be more involved in high school and that is obviously not the normal path you'd expect for a computer geek.

But, along with that, I was constantly getting into trouble with computers. Never with the cops, but I was always getting banned from all the computers in the school district. Then, they would let me back in, and I would mess up again for whatever reason. It happened over and over. I was caught in this dichotomy of trying to be involved, but whenever I was trying to get involved with computers, I messed it up because I was curious and experimenting outside what was allowed.

After that, I went to a small liberal arts college. I studied history along with computer science, because I knew ultimately I was going to work with computers and I wanted to learn something else, too. I studied Catholic history and the history of science, which overlap a lot. I'm not Catholic. I'm not a religious person at all, but it was really fascinating to learn all of the idiosyncrasies of Galileo and Bruno and all these different weird scientists who got burned at the stake for their discoveries.

I realized about probably three-quarters of the way through my education that in terms of computers, I actually wasn't learning anything I needed to learn to get a job later on. I did learn some coding concepts in college, but more importantly I figured out that I'm an experiential learner. I need to put my hands on things and really see them, and really chew on them. It was better to do it in a real context, where it mattered if I did it right. Like where there was money at stake. So, I did an internship in Iowa City, IA. I worked for a real company that was trying to make a profit. The company built ecommerce apps. As an intern I started learning web apps to build web pages.

Given my way of learning, it was fascinating to see how the management dealt with me. I was a child. I asked questions like a child does. "Why is the sky blue?" They just said, "It's just blue. Go with that." I said, "No! Tell me why we're doing it this way. What is this?" It was client services, so we were just doing it because the client wanted it done, with no thought behind it. But all the questions I asked gave me this opportunity to see how things worked and the value of asking things that seemed obvious to everyone else. It gave me a lot of hope. It really kicked off the career that I have now.

The methods I used to learn technology don't work for everything. I'm struggling with learning Japanese. My wife is Japanese and I want to learn the language, but I don't know how. I take classes, I fail, it doesn't work out. I have to figure that out. With technology, I immediately find a problem I want to solve. It's usually about learning a new programming language or learning a new technology. If it's a real problem, I want to get to where I can actually picture the solution and be able to see it through from the beginning to the end. For me, I can't learn from videos. That just doesn't do it for me, although there's a lot of video learning right now. I find it very frustrating. So usually what I do is I just go through a tutorial of some sort and then really start iterating, doing it over and over. I start trying to be creative on top of that, and say okay, now that I can figure out how to do this, how would I use it? So I set a new goal pretty close in difficulty, and when I achieve that, I do that again, until suddenly I've learned something. When you're in that process, it can also be the best time to teach someone else. A tech writer named Mark Pilgrim, who writes manuals for learning coding languages including *Dive into Python*, and *Dive into HTML5* said, "The best time to write a book about something is while you're learning it yourself." So you know what's hard to learn and can talk in an excited, confident, honest way about how you got to the place where it's not hard anymore.

For me this whole process is really collaborative. I treat everything like I'm the CEO of my life. CEOs have boards of directors and boards of advisors and these are groups of people who they're using to really rely on for help and advice to be successful. I think every person should treat their life like that.

So, if I'm stuck, I know I can reach out to a buddy, or I can reach out to my brother. I know I can reach out to these people who are experts in whatever I'm trying to do. I try to surround myself with incredibly smart people who are often, if not always, smarter than me. Because other people are so important to learning, I also think one of the most significant things about the internet is democratization of access. Anyone can email you about self-learning and you're probably going to respond. Probably. I think it's about how you phrase it. We are all very busy, but we're probably going to respond if you approach it efficiently.

You can learn a lot about this from a really good book called *Team Geek* by Brian W. Fitzpatrick. It's actually about project managing software development geeks, but it applies to most things with communication. It should really be called "Interacting with People," because all it is, is just little tricks on how to interact with people, how to make those interactions better.

There's a section called "Interacting with an Executive," and that part should be called "Interacting with Busy People." It says if you want to connect with someone who is very busy, tell them three bullets and then a call to action.

So if someone wanted help from me, it might go like this: "Harper, I'm interested in what you're doing with the campaign. I'm going to be doing technology for a campaign in the coming election. Do you have a hint for product management or project management software that you guys use?" I can answer that quickly. It's very simple. Then all of a sudden there's this person who probably wouldn't have had an opportunity to talk with me, and I can help them out. I love what that kind of efficient communication does for you.

Harper Reed's website is harperreed.org

Pablos Holman

"My strategy for learning has always been to take things apart and see how they work, and to see how you can manipulate them."

Pablos Holman *is a futurist, inventor, and notorious hacker with a unique view into breaking and building new technologies. He consults worldwide on invention and design projects that assimilate new technologies. He works at Intellectual Ventures, an innovation lab in Seattle. He is a high school graduate.*

Pablos tells the story of how he learned everything he knows by tinkering to see how things work and by learning on the job. He started as a computer hacker in childhood. His demonstrable skills and reputation got him jobs after high school. He says every job he's had has been an experience of getting paid to learn new things, and that as a businessperson, he's learned a great deal that's impossible to learn in school.

At Intellectual Ventures, where I work, we invent things. We have about 20 large-scale experiments running at any given time. We have a lab with one of every kind of scientist, and we bought one of every tool in the world, and stuck everybody on the same team. Our product is an invention. Usually that means that we invent something and patent it, which takes four to five years. We're on a longer timeline than most companies who have to ship a new product every year. So we get to work on things that are more futuristic.

My job specifically is to think about the application of new technologies, which also means my job is to be learning new things all the time. It's exciting when you get your hands on something new—which could be a new chip or a new sensor, or some new possibility that's been discovered in science. Every time, it's an opportunity to go reimagine everything that humans have ever done and see if this new capability lets us do it better. And you have to take it apart and learn how it works, and the contexts it could be used in, so that you can think about what it could be used for.

So far, I've worked on a brain surgery tool and a machine to suppress hurricanes. I tried to cure cancer, which didn't work. I worked on self-sterilizing elevator buttons. I didn't know anything about these areas before. What I'm good at is taking a project and an idea and just barreling through it to figure out if it's going to work. That skill set is applicable to anything. When I was working on the brain surgery tool, I had some of the world's leading brain surgery experts helping me out. When I was working on cancer, I was able to round up people who know all about cancer to help with the idea.

The researchers in our lab tend to be really specialized. We have a paleontologist, a nuclear physicist, laser experts, biochemical engineers, and doctors of various descriptions. I'm actually a specialist in computer hacking, but what I really bring to the job is being a good generalist who can see the possible connections between various specializations. That all comes from the way I educated myself. It comes particularly from not going to college, because I was never encouraged to specialize. Most of my education from elementary school on was characterized by the fact that I had a computer. That had nothing to do with school. I saw early on that learning outside school was valuable. I was the only one around who had a computer, so I spent most of my childhood on the computer, or trying to explain to people what I was doing on the computer.

I got an Apple II when I was 9 or 10. Computers in those days weren't really useful for anything. Certainly nothing that a 10-year-old kid needed to do. Mostly, I did a lot of things to figure out what the computer itself could do, what its limits were. It was this bottomless pit of intrigue. You had to really figure it out on your own. If you had a computer and you were doing this, what you did was collect software. Every new piece of software was a new superpower that you could strap on. I'd fire up those programs. I'd type every single command in and I'd run through every menu and figure out everything it could do. The volume of software on the market was low enough, I literally did that process with every single program ever made. For about a 20-year span, I used every program ever made to the extent that I acquired it, I fired it up, I clicked on everything and figured out what it could do, then moved on to the next one.

For example, I didn't play games—I gamed them. That was more interesting. There was a game called *Ultima*. Compared to today these were really rudimentary games, but essentially you're walking around in this *Dungeons & Dragons* type of world slaying dragons and stuff. There are always obstacles. Bodies of water was a big one. You'd run into an ocean, and to cross the ocean, you had to collect enough gold to buy a ship. What I did was to figure out how to read the map in the code the game was made of, and I would convert all the water to ships. Then you could just walk right across it. So my strategy for learning has always been to take things apart and see how they work, and to see how you can manipulate them.

When I got out of high school, instead of going to college, I figured out that companies would pay me to buy the hottest new computers on the market and try to make them do stuff for them. So I got all these consulting jobs just buying computers. I took those jobs because I wanted to get my hands on that hardware, which I couldn't afford. I got paid to learn. I went to work, I got hot new computers, I played, I learned on the job. I felt like I better not screw it up because an actual person had referred me to every one of those jobs. I was responsible to them socially as well as to the employer.

Through all the jobs I've had—my startups, and now working with Intellectual Ventures—other people have spent millions of dollars on the education I've gotten on the job. One of my favorite ways to learn is that I've been in factories all over the place as part of my work, and for speaking engagements. I do a lot of odd speaking engagements for that reason, because I get to go to bizarre places and see the inside of them. Recently, I went to Parma, Italy, to give a talk to the biggest pasta maker on earth. I got to visit this factory where they make the spaghetti that gets sold all over the world. I spent time with the Barilla brothers. It's their family business from several generations back. I got to ask them all types of questions about the history of the company, the factories, and how they do everything. They took me on private tours. You don't get to do that if you're an MBA student. I think of all that as my higher education. And it's better than an MBA.

I'm not an isolated example. A lot of the people I think of as being the most capable and accomplished are those that dropped out of college and learned what they do on the job. Learning that way gives you a sense of responsibility and a sense of ownership of your skills and knowledge in a way that a degree doesn't. You get a degree and it's an external authority saying you know what you're doing. The degree abstracts responsibility for learning and the knowledge you have.

What school doesn't do can be summed up as apprenticeship. You find a situation where you can go hang out with smarter people who know more than you. I think that's a pretty good formula for anybody's life. Surround yourself with people who are going to challenge you. Don't surround yourself with a bunch of average people, because then you're going to end up that way. You have to maximize your curiosity.

David Mason

"All these experiences learning on the job really changed the way I look at hiring people. I couldn't care less if you have a degree or not."

David Mason is currently the Director of Community Dynamics at New Kind, an agency working as community catalysts on brand, culture, and design. He's also played in a band, led a team of developers at Mozilla to build things on top of the Firefox platform, managed an international team of developers to create Red Hat Linux, been part of a tech team for a presidential campaign, and worked for an international public nonprofit building technologies for health workers in Africa. Being a musician is the only one of these jobs for which he had any formal training.

Dave got his first big job, at Red Hat, with a time-honored independent learning strategy: He said he knew how to do something he didn't, and then learned it really fast. What's important is that he had confidence he could learn it on his own, which changed his career options, and also his hiring practices as a manager. If you're concerned about getting a job without paper credentials, listen to Dave's idea of a qualified candidate.

DON'T GO BACK TO SCHOOL

This is something I don't really tell a lot of people, but now I don't really care because it has been so long. When I got hired at Red Hat, there wasn't an in-depth interview process. I met with the owner, Marc Ewing, and we were really just shooting the shit. He asked me if I knew anything about XML. I knew some about SGML but not really about XML yet. But I told him, "Yes, sure I do," because I knew that I could find out whatever I needed to know. I knew I could learn it. That was it. He showed me around the office and I was hired. It always felt a little disingenuous, but I was right. I could learn it and I did.

When I'd been at Red Hat for a year, I shifted from coding to managing coders. We reached a point where we needed management and we didn't nec-essarily have the funds yet to go out and hire experienced people. It fell to me because I was one of the few in engineering with good communication skills. It was important that I understood enough about programming to know what it takes to create products, put together teams, and get them to work together and meet goals.

I didn't know how to be a manager when I started doing it. Most of the learning came from trying things out. They would either blow up in my face or work. When I look back on some of the things that I did, I realize how dumb we were in handling certain situations. But I am also really proud of us. It's still really surprising to me that I do this for a living. I'm surprised that I understand it, that I'm gainfully employed doing it, and also that I'm so interested in it.

All these experiences learning on the job really changed the way I look at hiring people. I couldn't care less if you have a degree or not. Some of the peo-ple who have worked with me and for me who don't have degrees are actually better than the ones who do have degrees.

I realized that what's important is hiring people who are confident in their ability to go find information and to learn. I don't care if they actually know things or not when I hire them. The best programmers don't know everything, but they know how to quickly pick up whatever it is they need to do. You can become good at picking things up fast, mostly by doing it a lot. Of course, it's not something you can put on a résumé. The usual interview process is misera-ble at detecting it. But when I see it in someone, I know it instantly and I want to hire them.

David Mason works with newkind.com

SCIENCES

Luke Muehlhauser

"It has never been easier to learn without school."

**Luke Muehlhauser,** *a devoted autodidact, is a philoso-pher and the Executive Director of the Machine Intelligence Research Institute (formerly the Singularity Institute). He left behind a Christian high school and world-view for a secular college, and then chose to drop out and study science on his own.*

Luke is an advocate of independent learning and celebrates the resources that have recently become widely available to learn-ers outside universities. Here he describes his process for tackling new subjects and how the process of writing about his learning and sharing his ideas with his community is crucial to internalizing new knowledge and to keeping an objective perspective on it.

My education started out very badly with 12 years at a very small Christian school in Minnesota. The quality of education was quite poor, especially in the sciences, for reasons you might expect. The first page of the Bob Jones University Press biology textbook said that if you make observations that disagree with the Word of God, you should go with the Word of God. I went to community college and then transferred to the University of Minnesota. After a year, I was disillusioned by the value of what I was studying so I dropped out of university and instead went into the workforce. After I dropped out, I worked in IT in Los Angeles for two years, but at the same time was rapidly gobbling up all kinds of sciences on my own and finding that I learned a lot better as an autodidact. I began writing a blog about what I was learning, and was recognized for my knowledge and writing ability on issues that matter to the Singularity Institute. So I was invited to be a visiting fellow and then was hired as a researcher, and then a few months after that I was made executive director.

Skipping school or dropping out of school is obviously a decision that should be made on a case-by-case basis. You want to come out of your education with certain types of competencies and not a lot of debt. But it has never been easier to learn without school. There are so many resources to become a generally capable and smart person and there is no trouble doing it outside of the school system at all. Your education should amplify your curiosity by giving you the opportunity to pursue things that you actually care about, and learning outside of school is ideal for that. Try to learn as many things as possible and not be afraid to fail quickly and keep trying, or switch tracks. You'll get experience and valuable lessons in a variety of fields, and you'll occasionally stumble across things that you thought you were going to be bad at, and it turns out you're pretty good at.

I've been doing this long enough that my process for learning new things is pretty streamlined. If I want to answer a particular question or learn about a particular subject, I have a certain type of algorithm that is very efficient for coming to understand a new field of knowledge as quickly as possible. Basically the quickest way that I've found to come to a good understanding of a new subject—at least if it's science, math, or philosophy—is to find recent information about the subject. If I know the field well enough to know what the narrow subject I'm trying to learn about is then I will just look on Google Scholar for what are called "review articles" or "survey articles" that are in the last four years on that specific topic, and then I will read through all those articles. They are awesome because they provide an overview of the different relevant fields, adjacent fields, who some of the leading researchers are, what the standard results in the literature are, what the open questions are, and the bibliography which contains references to all of the experimental studies that led to the conclusions that are summarized in the review paper. A good review article (or two or five) on the subject is my best place to start. You also have to be careful not to just take what the review article says for granted. You have to look into the empirical basis and the experimental design of the studies that feed into those review articles. Were they conducted with solid methodology and proper controls?

If I don't know the field well enough to know even what the specific subject matter is called or what the key terms to search for are, I will often have to start with a university textbook on the broader subject and then flip through the chapters and try to find what the key terms are so I can search for them on Google Scholar.

The way my brain works for keeping track of these things is by summarizing and writing about the readings in my own words. That's the best way for me to keep it in my memory. It also happens to be a good way to share the results of your efforts with other people on the internet, especially if you're part of a community that's investigating a particular topic. You can share your findings with others, post those results, and then maybe people will post back and say, "That's great, but did you see this study that had a different result? What do you think of that?" Maybe they can point to things that you had not even found.

Most people assume you need a PhD to publish in peer-reviewed books and journals, but it's not true—I've published in peer-reviewed venues without even a bachelor's degree, because I learned the material well enough on my own to engage at the cutting edge of human knowledge.

Luke Muehlhauser's website is <u>lukeprog.com</u>

Zack Booth Simpson

"*In a way, the best education you can get is just talking with people who are really smart and interested in things, and you can get that for the cost of lunch.*"

 **Zack Booth Simpson** *is a software engineer, artist, and molecular biology researcher at the University of Texas at Austin. Without any formal study in the sciences, he's contributed to over half-a-dozen scientific papers published in peer-reviewed academic journals. Zack is a high school dropout.*

Zack struggled with formal school—even at its best, he felt it worked against his natural curiosity and love of learning by taking away his autonomy. His school experiences show a marked contrast with the satisfaction and self-sufficiency he experienced working and learning on the job in a variety of situations in his youth. He has a long history of getting jobs without formal credentials. One of my favorite things about talking to Zack is his conviction that the way he's approached learning is a "perfectly viable way for anyone to do it." He says people often feel he's been successful in spite of his unconventional path because he's somehow exceptional. He thinks they've got it all backward. "Maybe it was the path that I took that made me extraordinary and not the other way around."

I was dyslexic, so I was really slow to learn to read, and I was very visually oriented, which school wasn't. For example, in first grade, the class was making a Thanksgiving dinner out of construction paper. The teacher asked if I wanted to make the turkey, but I thought that was way too hard. I said I'd make the cranberry sauce. I took a giant pile of construction paper, and the teacher said—in what I now know was a sarcastic tone—"Are you sure that will be enough?" So then, without paying attention to what anybody else was doing, I made my cranberry sauce. It was all put up on the bulletin board in time for parent-teacher conferences. My mom came in and pointed straight at mine—she knew it was mine. It was 3D, not 2D. Now you see why I didn't want to make the turkey!

I started playing with computers when I was eight or nine. When I was about 12, I used to go to a little mom-and-pop store that sold software for the computer I had, a TRS-80. I really liked this little store. One day I was in there with my mom and I said it would be so fun to work there. She told me to ask the owners. It never had occurred to me. She said, "Put on some nice clothes, walk in, and ask if you could have a job." I did that and they hired me. They paid me $2.00 an hour under the table and it was great. When I started, I did little things like filing and cleaning. They saw that I could help customers, so I started fixing computers and installing software for people. By high school I was something like an assistant manager. So from an early age, I had a job in a real store where they expected me to act as an adult. Having a responsible job at that early age really shaped who I am.

In high school, things really fell apart. I went to a magnet school that was created on the East Side of Austin, which was terrible. My father talked me into trying a boarding school. It was a beautiful place with nurturing people. But I was still just as turned off by being ordered to learn particular things and not having my own time to learn what I wanted. I'm really naturally interested in learning things, but there's one way to guarantee that I lose interest, and that's to tell me to be interested in it, even if I am. So, school worked against my natural instinct to learn. After one trimester at the boarding school, they suggested I could leave, and I didn't want to be there anymore anyway.

When I went back to Austin, I needed another job so I could still be independent and not too much of a drain on my mom. I heard about a job typing quality assurance reports at a software company. I went to an interview, and there had been some kind of miscommunication. They thought I was applying for the quality assurance job, not for the data entry job. I didn't correct them. The quality assurance job was basically a junior programming job, since to do quality assurance on the compiler, you had to write programs to test the compiler. I thought, that's fine—I know how to program, I can do that too.

I did that while I was supposedly finishing my junior year back at public high school. There was a specific moment when I realized it didn't make sense for me to be there. I was in Spanish class in a windowless interior room taught by some teacher that didn't speak Spanish. She was a first-year teacher. That day she handed out a Spanish word jumble puzzle—the busiest of busywork ever. When you're a student, you're like a robot: Someone puts something down in front of you, you just mindlessly do it. That day, what I thought was, I could write a program to optimize this search. If I had been at work, I would have been paid to have that idea. Somehow I had learned what first-year teachers' salaries were and I realized that my salary was bigger than her salary. I thought, what am I doing? I'm just sitting here doing busywork for this woman who makes less money than I make, who isn't teaching me anything, and I'm wasting my brain when I could be working and getting paid for this. So I just stopped showing up after that. I went to work full-time for that database company. I worked there for five years.

A friend of mine was working for a game company and it sounded a lot more fun, so I applied there and was hired. Within a few years, when I was 22 or 23, I was the director of technology there. What had really paid off in terms of my career was that I had two skills that I had managed to build for myself. One was programming, which I taught myself and did for fun, and the other one was acting like a professional adult. Eventually I started making interactive artwork for science and children's museums. That turned out really well for paying my bills, so I had the luxury of doing what I wanted to do for a while. And what I wanted to do was sit around reading textbooks.

In those days, my girlfriend and I both worked out of the house. At lunchtime, we'd meet up in the kitchen and I'd tell her about, let's say, the thermodynamics textbook I was reading, and she'd tell me about the web page she was designing. After a while, she told me that I needed more nerd friends.

We lived near the University of Texas. She said why don't you go down there and talk to them about going to grad school? I made an appointment with a graduate advisor and he asked what my degree was in. I told him I didn't have one. In fact, I didn't even have a high school diploma.

He said, well, you need a GED, and then you go get an undergraduate degree, and then come on back in. That wasn't going to happen. It was ridiculous to me. But one good thing came out of it: I had told him I was interested in the intersection of biology and computation. He said that I should talk to Professor Edward Marcotte, who is a computational biologist.

I went to see Edward and we hit it off right away. He knew my artwork and he had played my video games and he had no preconceived notions of what I did or didn't know. He walked me around the lab and pointed to every piece of equipment and explained how cool it was. He was infectiously positive. As I was leaving he asked what I wanted to work on. I said honestly that I just wanted to hang out and learn stuff. He said okay, great, there's the desk right there, we meet on Wednesdays. That was it. That's how I started working in his lab.

At first, I was a little worried I'd be a leech on the system, asking dumb questions. I really wanted to be able to contribute. I knew I could at least be useful because I know computers, and people everywhere, at every level, end up needing help with that. I was totally wrong to have worried—the first thing I learned was that there are no dumb questions. Not only that, it was not uncommon that a grad student would thank me later for asking something, because they didn't feel like they could ask. In the same way, my fear that all I would be able to contribute would be essentially IT help was completely wrong. My contribution was the fact that I had a radically different view on everything that was being discussed. I had read the same textbooks, but I hadn't sat in on the classes. I just had a very different way of looking at the material. The reason I have a different perspective is because I didn't go to school. I didn't go the route they took. Ironically, my value to them is exactly the fact that I didn't do what they all did.

Here's an example: Shortly after I started, Edward and I were walking down the hall and he mentioned an MIT contest in synthetic biology engineering. We went to the planning meeting. The professor who was running it was Andy Ellington, who I didn't know at the time, but he's since become a really good friend. He was reading the contest description, which asked entrants to build a state machine out of bacterial cells. He asked everyone, "What the hell's a state machine?" No one knew what a state machine was except me. I said state machines are really cool, here I'll explain it. It turned into a whole lesson about computational theory.

What we wanted to do was choose an algorithm that when multiplied by a gigantic number of bacteria would do something interesting. I proposed making a bacterial edge detector. The idea was to engineer real bacteria to behave in a certain way. So you lay the bacteria on an agar plate, and project an image down onto the plate—let's say a checkerboard. The bacteria will compute where the edges are and then respond to indicate if they're at a boundary between light and dark, for example, forming a checkerboard grid. I made the algorithm for it, but I didn't know the chemistry. I knew it was possible, but I didn't know how exactly. Everyone thought it was a cool idea and started to talk through how it would work. They explained the chemistry to me and I explained the computation to them.

Over the course of the next year, with a lot of collaboration from Chris Voigt's lab at the University of California at San Francisco, we built the state machine. My contribution was having this radically different perspective from the trained scientists. It was the fact that I didn't know all that chemistry, because if I had, I might not have proposed the project. Because the chemistry was really hard.

I feel now actually a little less creative in the lab than I did five years ago, because I now know a lot of the chemistry and biology better. I talk myself out of ideas very quickly when I don't see right away how to implement them. Early on, I was more creative because I didn't know what wasn't possible.

My experience is not as uncommon as you might think. Edward Marcotte was particularly open to it, but it happens from time to time. From the outside, it's easy to think of a university as a big, tall building with a set of steps that lead up the front, and some guards at the top of those steps to keep you out. But, if you look around the side of the building, there are a whole bunch of doors that are wide open! Not every professor is like this, but there are a lot of professors who welcome it. They like having people around who are interested in things.

As far as education goes, some people talk as if lecturers have a magic wand that downloads information into your head. But it's your job to learn it, not somebody else's to download it to you. You have to read the book. You have to think through what the lecturer is saying. I think everyone is an autodidact.

For me, there are three ways of learning. Reading, listening to lectures, and having smart friends. As to reading, when I get interested in an area of science, I start by reading a popular-science book. Those are usually well written, in a way that you can understand without any expertise. Then I move on to textbooks. There are two important things about reading a textbook. One is don't sweat it; if you don't understand something, so what, keep reading. Two is that no one retains everything, even someone who gets a PhD in the subject. Textbooks are for getting the gist of something and then having a reference that you can go back to when you need it.

A deeper part of learning is having friends. I have a lot of smart friends. As I started hanging out at the lab, I started getting a lot more smart friends. My friend's grandmother told him a joke. She said don't marry for money, just hang out with rich people and marry for love. My addendum to that is don't bother getting an education, just hang out with smart people and ask good questions.

There are people like Edward and Andy from the University of Texas, and my neighbor John, who is a professor of electrical engineering. I ask questions of them all the time. I go to lunch with them and we just have great conversations. In a way, the best education you can get is just talking with people who are really smart and interested in things. You can get this education for the cost of lunch. For a lot of professors, there's nothing they like more than talking about whatever the hell it is that they work on. You can just cold-call a professor who does research you're interested in. Read up on it first, and then call and say, "Hey, can I take you to lunch, I'm thinking about such and such." Not everyone will respond, but a fair number will.

Having smart friends is definitely a key to maintaining your motivation, and smart friends are also free. The important thing is being able to give something back. Friendships aren't one way. What's surprising is how much people get out of just talking with somebody who asks good questions. Even a professor whose work you don't understand in detail, if you're excited about it and you're interested enough to ask good questions, then you're actually contributing to their work because you're making them think about what they're doing. You're making them answer basic questions without resorting to jargon.

I can imagine a more organized way of learning this way, where you start with X amount of dollars and go to lunch every day with a professor, while reading textbooks. It will cost you maybe $1,000 to have the best education that you can imagine. I did this by happenstance, but I don't see why one couldn't plan it out and do it that way on purpose.

Zack Booth Simpson's website is <u>mine-control.com/zack</u>

EXTRA CREDIT

Karen Barbarossa

"There is a lot of literature on the best language-learning processes but no one taught me that, not really, not when I started absorbing languages."

 **Karen Barbarossa** *is a product designer and a writer. She is also a lover of languages and an avid student of language, culture, and context. Unlike many of the people I interviewed for this book, Karen has two graduate degrees, one in language and one in business. Karen understands more than a dozen languages. She has learned them through classes, by independent means, and by traveling. She has also taught English as a second language. In and out of school, she learned how to best learn new languages quickly and easily. Here she shares her approaches and experiences.*

As a child, foreign languages seemed like the doors to worlds of magic. My grandparents spoke an Italian dialect my brothers and I didn't understand, a language of secrets. I don't remember if I was exposed to other spoken languages when I was young, but I was a curious and voracious reader, and I can remember being aware of other worlds, places, and other languages I read about. As I got older and began to learn languages, they did open up new worlds. I loved the light they shine on culture, context, how people feel, and think. The stories people tell me seem different, depending on the language and country.

I think part of why people teach themselves things is based on fascination or passion or some other internal force that drives them to it. For me, it's the drive to know and experience the whole world. To really understand a language and how it works also means understanding the history of the language, the history of the land, the people, and the geography. If I could spend all my time wandering around in the world, spending months at different places learning languages, I would do that.

There is a lot of literature on the best language-learning processes but no one taught me that, not really, not when I started absorbing languages. Later I found out that what I learned matched a lot of research on language learning. But for me, I figured it out on my own. It's not the same for everyone, and that's important. You have to try different ways and see what sticks. For example, I found that I can't learn a language I can't read. So I have had to learn all kinds of alphabets, whereas my brother doesn't need to read, he can learn by hearing. I know I will have to put in extra time, in the beginning, because if I can't see the language I can't seem to store it in my head. But the basics of learning a language seem pretty similar for most people.

It's easier to learn a language in a place where it is spoken, whether that's another country or an enclave in your town. There are parts of language learning that I do use textbooks for. Word order, verb order, does the language have declensions, are there masculine and feminine words, and so on. Gendered words are not the same gender across all languages. It's not as though if you know the moon is feminine in one language, she will maintain her femininity everywhere. It doesn't work like that, which is a shame. Each one has to be memorized separately. After the textbooks, I talk to everyone who will talk to me. I listen to everyone who is speaking. The radio, the television, train announcements, anything. This is where a fluent speaker can make it more pleasant. Then you just turn to them and ask questions. Strangers are nice about this too, if you are sitting in a café and ask someone to explain a word to you, that helps.

Really, the best possible way to learn a language for me is to have someone at my beck and call who's fluent in that language. Because basically I'll pester them, "So how do you say this? Is this right? What if I wanted to say this?" And I often ask how to say very absurd things because if I can do that, then I really understand the structure. The absurdity is part of the fun, as well, the laughter at the ridiculous things that are grammatically correct but silly. When I was learning Hebrew, I was talking with a friend about hamburgers and meat, and the different ways of talking about meat in Hebrew. I asked, "If I wanted to say that I wanted an elephant hamburger with ketchup, would I say it like this?" He just looked at me funny and said, "Yes, it's exactly like that." So I knew I understood it, I understood the structure well enough to use it. Once I understand the framework, I can plug in the words, but without the framework, the grammatical model, you're just throwing words around willy-nilly.

I listen to a lot of radio, often in languages I don't speak. They start to make sense after a while. It's a very passive type of learning, the intonation and structure float into me, the music and texture of the language, even if I am not understanding what is being said, yet. It soaks around and it's really useful when I start speaking, because I've been listening to the accent.

One of my professors in school said you should never learn a language alone and don't sit at the table and learn the language because you will never remember a language sitting alone at a table. He was keen on contextual learning. That's been my experience. I used to do things like listen to language tapes while washing dishes. One thing I discovered is that I cannot listen to language tapes and drive a car well. I don't know what's going on in my brain, and at the last moment I have to save myself from veering off the road or into another car.

I've also found that learning languages in school often makes them less functional in the real world, because you learn a formal, polite version of a language in classes, not languages as they are spoken. For example, when I lived in Switzerland I watched American movies, dubbed in French and subtitled in French as well. Ones with really foul language, such as *Magnolia* and *American Beauty*. I got all this raunchy slang from the subtitles.

When I moved to Washington, DC, I lived with one of my brothers, who also knows many languages. We decided to learn a language together that neither of us spoke, which turned out to be a funny process of elimination. We were down to Arabic or Brazilian Portuguese. We decided to go with Portuguese because I wanted to dance, and we thought it would be easier and faster to learn. We took a class together and spoke Portuguese together at home for about three months. We butchered it at times, but we'd look things up, too. It's great when you have a partner in crime for learning languages.

Not too long ago I was doing some consulting on contextual linguistics and translation, and I found a chart showing how the State Department teaches languages. What they'd found from their studies was pretty spot on for what I've learned by trying it out for myself.

I think the biggest thing though, is that this is fun. Every language is a new mystery, so it's completely exciting when I get to embark on another one. Even thinking about it now, I can't wait to start on a new one, to get out there, to begin again.

Cory Doctorow

"The more you can be objective about your work, the better. You learn to do that by learning to critique other people's work first."

 **Cory Doctorow** *is a science fiction author, activist, jour-nalist, and blogger—the co-editor of* <u>boingboing.net</u> *and the author of Tor Teen/HarperCollins UK novels such as* For the Win *and the best-selling* Little Brother. *He is the former European director of the Electronic Frontier Foundation and cofounded the UK Open Rights Group. He attended seven years of high school and dropped out of four universities. He holds an honorary doctorate in computer science from the Open University in the UK.*

For people who want to teach themselves to write, Cory offers a detailed portrait of what got him into writing, how he started teaching himself, how he gets work done as a writer, and the practicalities of being a working writer. One effective way to learn creative writing is to participate in a writing group or workshop. Instead of an MFA program, read Cory's explanation of how to run a productive group and how working with a group teaches you about writing.

Writing, for me, started when I was six. This was 1977, and the ability of a six-year-old to experience narratives was pretty constrained. We only had three TV channels. We didn't have a DVD player, obviously. We didn't have a VCR. And we didn't have YouTube. The books I had were children's books. But I saw *Star Wars*. *Star Wars* is not the most complicated story, but it's got multiple points of view. It has nonlinear storytelling. It was, I think, the most complicated story I'd ever seen. It really got me sort of fizzing. You know, this idea of a story that was more than just the linear, single point-of-view narrative. I went home and I tried to take it apart the same way that you would try and take apart and reconstruct a toy that you were interested in. I got some paper, stapled it down the side, trimmed it to the size of a mass-market paperback, and wrote out the story of *Star Wars* as best as I could remember. The exercise was so exciting and just felt so good that I announced on the spot that I wanted to write books. And I kept it up. Then, for a while, I wanted to be an astronaut and a deep-sea diver and all the rest of it.

I went back to writing, and when I was 16, I decided I was going to try to commercialize my work. I started writing stories and sending them to magazines. At 17, I made my first semi-professional sale. Ten years later, I made my first professional sale. Five more years after that, my first novel came out. Learning to write isn't just about learning to tell good stories, it's about learning how to do your work and sell your work.

As a writer, just doing your work is something a lot of people struggle with. I did too. My solution was that I started writing even when I didn't feel like it. I started writing even when I felt like I was writing bad material. I chose a modest word count goal and did it every day, in narrative sequence. At the time, when I was working full days for the Electronic Frontier Foundation, it was 250 words a day, which is a page. A page a day is a novel year. Even on the most blocked up, miserable day, it only took 45 minutes to write 250 words. Most days, it took 15 minutes. Anyone can find 15 minutes in a day. Even after my daughter Poesy was born, and my wife, Alice, and I were running around like chickens with their heads cut off, there was 15 minutes sometime in the day. The discipline of writing every day and the habit of writing every day made it a lot easier.

If you write every day just a little bit, in sequence, it just becomes a thing you do. It becomes much easier to do it even on days when you don't feel like doing it, and especially on days when you're not feeling it. I used to think of writing as such a major undertaking, something that required so much mental preparation and physical preparation—you know, the right music, a cigarette, whatever. Breaking that habit, turning writing into something mundane, makes it slightly less satisfying, maybe. But it's also a lot less misery-making. Taking the heroism out of writing was a huge thing.

To figure out what I'm writing each day, I tend to work with major signposts in the narrative. At least the next two or three known things. I like to think of it as a journey where you've got three or four errands you need to run. I've got three or four places I need the story to go. Each place has to have the character or characters in greater peril with a bigger problem to solve. The character tries to solve her problem, fails through no fault of her own, and things get worse.

As long as you're doing that on every page, you will get to a point of higher tension, and there will be a reason for the reader to keep reading. This way, it's really easy to figure out where you should go next. You think: What would make the situation worse? How can this person try to solve this problem, fail, and have things get worse? It doesn't have to be like I diffuse a bomb and there is a bigger bomb underneath it. It can be: I got into an argument with someone and tried to sort it out and actually offended them more.

One of my favorite resources for these kinds of stories is Dale Carnegie's *How to Win Friends and Influence People*, because it's a book written for socially inept people who can't figure out why no one likes them. If you reverse his advice, every situation that Dale Carnegie talks about is a road map for how to alienate people and make your social circumstance worse. All you need to do is do the opposite of everything Dale Carnegie says, and you will have a character who does things that people really do in the real world. You and your readers will feel like you can understand why they would do these things because we've all done them. That is a way of making things worse in a social way.

Another thing that's hard is getting myself back into it every day. My best technique for that is leaving off in the middle of a sentence where you know what the rest of the sentence is going to be. Because that way, you can write the first three or four words without having to be creative. And then you're already being creative. And then you're already writing. Another thing to avoid is when you get to a point where you could stop and do something fairly noncreative and distracting for a while to fix the story. So you've got a spear carrier who needs to have a name. You could open the phone book. You could do lots of things. But the actual character's name isn't particularly important to the story; they just need to have a name. This is where you just write "TK," which is what journalists do. And then you go back to it later. Or, anytime you've got a fact that you're pretty sure of that you want to make sure is right, you do that too. Like, how long is the Brooklyn Bridge? The Brooklyn Bridge, all 800 feet of it, across whatever river it is. I can't even remember what river the Brooklyn Bridge goes over. You just write "FCK," fact check.

What's great is you don't have to go to an MFA program to learn these skills. You can learn them in a well-run writing group. While it's nice to have six weeks with an instructor in the formal program, the major value that you get out of being in a writing workshop is critiquing people who are at about the same level as you, not receiving wisdom from on high. This is something anybody can set up for themselves. Just get a group together and agree on the ground rules. From day to day and week to week, I don't even think it's good to have a mentor who reads everything you write and tells you what's good and what isn't. I think having input from unprivileged viewpoints, everyone being equal, is much better. The main thing that group critiquing does is it gives you a better critical eye for your own work. To me, learning to critique is more important than receiving critique. I think every writer goes into a writing workshop at the start feeling like what they want is to improve a particular story by getting some critical feedback; or, if they're really honest with themselves, they also want someone to tell them they're brilliant.

But the best stuff that you can get out of it is learning to turn a cold, rational eye on your own work in pretty short order. Your goal is to have the experience of putting something in a drawer and coming back to it later and being able to look at it with fresh eyes and saying "Aha. I can fix that, I can fix that, I can fix that." The shorter that drawer period can be, the better. The more you can be objective about your work, the better. You learn to do that by learning to critique other people's work first.

One thing to look out for is that writing workshops can hurt writers by making it hard to separate the urge to revise from the urge to compose. You have to figure out how to stop critiquing yourself while you're writing, and come back to critiquing when you're done. You can't revise and compose at the same time. It's the centipede dilemma. You know, "Hey Mr. Centipede, how do you walk with all those feet?" "I don't know," he says. "I've never thought about it." And he never walks again.

There are important ground rules to running a good group. Everybody has to submit. Sometimes a member stops writing but doesn't stop coming to the workshop. If you're not submitting to the workshop you lose the right to critique. People form groups without any mechanism for un-forming them. Without establishing a formal process for ejecting someone from the workshop—and having it exist prior to behaving in ways that make them no longer a candidate for the workshop—you end up in a mean-spirited thing where now we've invented a rule that means you can't come anymore, as opposed to everyone agreeing at the start that anyone who hasn't submitted a manuscript in six months is out, or at least annually if they're doing novels.

Another point about work in progress: I really strongly believe that it's better to have a workshop in which the manuscripts are given well in advance than one in which the manuscripts are handed out at the start of the workshop. Having a long fuse for critique is better. It's better if you can read it a couple of times.

Unless it's really a big deal, don't critique punctuation, grammar, and spelling, just mark it. There's nothing more deadly than being in a group of 18 people and listening to someone speak at length about someone else's commas. That's the kind of thing that you can just circle in red ink in a manuscript. By all means circle it, give the manuscript back to the writer, but you don't need to talk about it. Talk about substantive issues. Don't repeat anything anyone else has said. Just say I agree with so-and-so. From there it's wide open because why a story works is as diverse and personal as why someone is likable.

For myself, I don't mind and I actually encourage specific rewrite suggestions. I think there are some writers who like hearing "this is broken" or "this is good," but saying you should fix it this particular way is unwelcome. But I think that specific rewrites are great. I think sometimes it's hard to express why you think something is broken, but in describing how you think it would be better, you can convey what you think is missing. It doesn't mean the writer has to take your suggestion, but it does have an information richness that's missing from a mere "this is broken" critique.

The other thing that is absolutely off-limits is critiques of the writer and not critiques of the work: "You always do this," "You're a misogynous prick for writing this," or "This is the technological optimism that you always do because you are such a naïve technophile." That kind of thing is absolutely off-limits.

There's a corollary to it that's never enforced which is that praise should be for the manuscript and not the writer: "This is me. This is my story. They're problems with my story. They're not problems with me." The corollary really should be: "This is me. This is my story. The virtues of my story are not virtues of me," but no one ever does that. If you're going to be really intellectually honest, you have to admit that the virtues in your story are not necessarily present in you. That's the reason that wife-beating assholes like Tolstoy could make good art because virtues can be an art that aren't in the artist.

This way of doing things can be so much better than an MFA. I have a friend who wanted to be a science fiction writer who went to the University of

Southern California creative writing program for thousands of dollars a year and who was only allowed to write one science fiction story in four years. The entire commercial advice she got from the program was jokes about how poor she was going to be. She didn't learn how to prepare a manuscript, how to research a market, how to find an accountant who understands the arts, how to incorporate a personal business to insulate yourself from liability if you ever get sued over one of your stories. None of that stuff was present in that academic program. Those are really important things to know.

I don't know that every creative writing program is like that, but I think that if you're considering graduate education in creative writing, you have to ask yourself: Will they let you write the kind of stories that you want to write, and also give you models for how to live a writer's life? Not just commercial models, but personal models like how do you live with a spouse when you have a career in the arts and they have a career that's a regular job—all of the soup to nuts of having a creative life. Unless you think you're going to come out of that program understanding how a writer lives, how a writer makes a living, how to write, and unless you're allowed to write the stuff that you want to, then you should run fast in the other direction.

Cory Doctorow's website is craphound.com

HOW TO BE AN INDEPENDENT LEARNER

How to Be an Independent Learner

Choose a learning method

Think about your favorite, most successful learning experiences and what characterized them. Try to recall experiences in a similar category of learning: skills, academic knowledge, crafts, etc. You might realize that you prefer to learn in different ways about areas of knowledge, such as environmental science, and skills, such as drawing.

The nuances to preferred ways of learning are plentiful, but they boil down to two broadly defined approaches:

- You learn new things with the goal of gaining mastery and understanding in a specific area of knowledge.
- Or, you guide your process by learning what you need to complete a specific project.

Within either of these approaches, you will also need to explore the learning strategies that are most effective for you. Strategies are ways of acquiring knowledge: reading, listening to lectures, discussing your subject with others, explaining or teaching what you're learning, collaborating on learning projects, attending workshops, taking online or in-person classes. This is where you want to think back to what has worked for you in the past, or try something new if you haven't found success with any of the methods you've already tried. These strategies are the tools by which you'll learn what you're interested in, and in all likelihood you'll use a combination of strategies.

Paths to general knowledge

First let's talk about learning an area of knowledge. To do this, you can follow one of two paths through the material: linear or associative.

A linear strategy follows a trajectory like traditional classroom learning, using a textbook, a syllabus, or an entire curriculum that is mapped out in an orderly way. This is a good choice if you have decided that you want to learn a subject as a whole, because the subject area is appealing to you, or it's something you wish you had learned in school. It also works well if you find classroom learning appealing, but want to do it outside of school. The main thing is the idea that you're eager to learn an entire subject area, a large body of knowledge.

Here's a picture of what a linear path looks like: You have decided that you want to learn basic physics. You can start by finding an introductory course online, or reading an introductory textbook, and learn the material in a commonly taught sequence of concepts. Newton's laws, motion, gravity, and so on, concepts that build on each other. The path through the material is straight and orderly. Completing established levels of advancement through the trajectory gives you a sense of accomplishing what you set out to learn.

By contrast, an associative path can start anywhere, and it often appears that you are starting smack in the middle, or even at the end of a classical learning trajectory. You become curious about something and work your way around the ideas you need to know to understand it. You skim over things that are too advanced, or back up until you find a level you understand, and go forward again. You will probably end up with an understanding of the subject that is deeper in some ways and shallower in others. It's an equally valid style, and it feels more natural to some learners. It tends to emerge from a specific curiosity rather than a desire for knowledge in general. Because it is driven by specific curiosity, it can be easier to follow through on. People who operate this way gain a satisfactory level of understanding of their original starting point and often move on to focus on one of the tangents that came out of their starting question. This works best for people who don't need a clear sense of completion, as there are an infinite number of tangents.

If you're new to independent learning, you may not be very familiar with what an associative path might look like, so I'll describe in some detail how this would look, again with the example of learning physics. Let's say you read a handful of articles about the Large Hadron Collider, a massive particle accelerator that is expected to discover new particles that exist in theory but have never been observed experimentally. Now you want to learn more about particle physics. You don't feel the need to be able to understand and calculate every formula or equation involved; you simply want to understand the area in a general way. If you started with an introductory physics textbook, it would take at least a few semesters' worth of learning before you get to the meat of particle physics.

Alternatively, an associative path might begin with reading the Wikipedia article on particle physics, or glancing at the table of contents of a particle physics textbook. You'll see from there that you need to understand the particles present in an atom and how they interact, so you find an introductory physics lecture online that explains the atom. From the textbook or Wikipedia article you would follow a path to gain a basic descriptive understanding of quantum mechanics. This might lead you to something called the Standard Model, which is a giant equation to account for the forces that hold atoms together (and by consequence, the universe). In order to work, the Standard Model requires the existence of particles that haven't been observed, and that's what scientists are looking for in their experiments with the Large Hadron Collider. A book about physics oriented toward a general audience and general audience talks by physicists you can find online can help you understand all of this. By following the tangents you need to understand what's going on at the Large Hadron Collider, you've arrived at a general understanding of a segment of physics. You've likely skipped basic Newtonian physical laws, but if you find that you need to learn them, you can go learn the elementary equations to describe things like force and motion. You've gone through the frustrations of having to find your own way and the degree of backtracking and restarting that can be involved. You may have giant gaps in your knowledge. You may have a more nuanced understanding of what you've learned. Either way, you're empowered and satisfied from having found your own way.

Project-driven learning

Learning by doing a project is a more focused learning experience than learning a body of general knowledge, and has a built-in means for keeping you motivated and marking your successes. It's the most common approach among independent learners. Doing a project gives you a defined goal and a sense of progress when you finish the project. The project puts your new skills and knowledge in an immediate context. You may use traditional assignments and exercises to hone skills or internalize knowledge, but they're in pursuit of something concrete, rather than material in a vacuum. Your project might be making a film, a physical object, a computer program, a science experiment, a book, a business, a graphic novel—anything that puts your learning in an active context and makes it useful.

These kind of concrete projects don't obviously apply to every area of knowledge. One of the best tricks I've heard independent learners talk about is turning their pursuit of a naturally abstract subject—such as philosophy or the history of art—into a concrete project. Often, the project involves sharing knowledge with others. You might go about this by making a film, recording a podcast, writing a blog about what you're learning, writing an article, making a graphical representation of your work, teaching a workshop, or running a reading group.

To learn in the context of a project, you're going to use many of the same strategies described for classroom-style learning, but you'll attach them to an achievable goal. You'll define your project and then make a list of what you think you need to learn to accomplish it. You'll seek out the knowledge and skills you need by some combination of the same methods described above: reading, listening, discussing, taking notes, collaborating, using tutorials, experimenting, and finding experts to help you.

Learning independently involves not being afraid of failure and do-overs. If you get started and find that the approach isn't working for you, see if you can reconfigure your approach by paying attention to what didn't work the first time. The key here is that if it's not working, try tinkering with your method using any of the different approaches described in this section of the book. Everyone I talked to reported that the process of coming to learn how they as individuals do their learning was one of the most significant advantages of learning outside of school. It also led to greater satisfaction with their experience and a deeper understanding of their material or skills. So be prepared for some experimentation!

Find learning resources

Finding the materials and resources you need is a much simpler process than finding your approach to learning. You'll be heavily dependent on your search engine skills, so it may take a little practice. Below I provide some hints about how to conduct searches and get help deciding which are the most effective or high-quality materials to use. You can refer to the **Resources** section of the book for places to start, but your own searches will also be vital, since there are new materials available every day.

Syllabi

A syllabus is the learning path established by a professor for their students to learn a particular subject during a semester. It lists the books required, the topics covered in each lecture, and often the criteria for success in the course. At some schools all classes are required to post their syllabi, and at others it's voluntary on the part of the professor. Some schools don't allow public access to these materials. Once you start exploring, you'll get a good sense of where and how to find a helpful syllabus. It's a good idea to compare a few and decide which seems most clear and compelling.

Some basic advice for discovering syllabi:

■ Search for "syllabi database"; try including or omitting your subject area to narrow or broaden your search.

- Search at particular universities. The syllabi database for Emory University is a good example: is.gd/6jmdto.
- Search for a course in a specific subject (e.g., Physics 101 or German history); you'll find syllabi from many schools.
- Search for open courseware materials, which can be good sources for syllabi, whether or not you use the lectures or other features.

Textbooks

If you want to use a textbook, your goal will be to find one that is respected by teachers, that students find useful and comprehensible, and that you can afford. There are a few good sources for that information. You can look for course syllabi from reputable schools and find out which textbooks they assign. You can also look on a website such as ask.metafilter.com; first search for "best [subject] textbook" and see if anyone has asked the question before. Chances are someone has, and you'll find suggestions from many knowledgeable people and explanations of why they endorse one book over another. If you don't find an existing thread, you can ask the question yourself if you're interested in joining the community.

Some collaborative learning communities keep their own lists of reliable sources. For example, one of my interviewees is part of a community focused on psychology and cognitive science. They have a section listing the best textbooks on everything people in the community know about, with specific criteria for nominating a textbook (see **Resources**, p. 179). You can find good material in a place like that, and also get a solid understanding of what kind of people are reliable sources of textbook reviews (e.g., someone who has read more than one). Amazon reviews are sometimes helpful if you can determine that the contributor has some level of knowledge about the topic. Students may also comment on the accessibility of a textbook, which is useful too.

Textbooks are expensive, but you can usually get a back edition for the price of a paperback novel. If the 10th edition is the most recent and costly (often hundreds of dollars), look for the 9th edition. Not that much will have changed; the textbook industry is invested in updating frequently for profitability as much as for keeping current with advancing knowledge.

Lectures

Many independent learners find that online lectures are a really effective way to learn new material. For any subject you're interested in, you'll want to try out lectures by a few different scholars or experts. Lecturing is a performance-based activity, and not all of the people who do it are gifted performers. If they're not, you're likely to lose interest quickly, not for lack of interest in your topic.

Skills-based tutorials are also plentiful and mostly free on the web. Check the **Resources** section of this book for some of the more reputable sources. You can also search to find text or video tutorials created by generous individuals, and it's a process of trial and error to find the tutorial producers who make the most sense to you. Taking a one-minute peek can usually give you a reliable sense of whether a tutorial producer is a competent, good communicator and teacher.

Online educational institutions

Online educational institutions range from small-group university classes for enrolled students conducted online to the MOOCs described in the introduction. Both differ from open courseware by attempting to more closely replicate the classroom experience, including conducting courses during a set time period, with automatically- or peer-evaluated assignments, and weekly work that must be done on schedule. Some MOOCs use discussion forums to encourage student participation and discussion, while traditional-scale online classes often use chat with other students and the instructor. Some MOOCs offer various types of certification, and some are moving toward granting college credits.

You'll find a list of MOOC platforms and open education options in the **Resources** section, p. 179.

Libraries

Beyond textbooks, your independent reading, research, and exploration will likely lead you to crave access to books in general: how-to books for technical and craft skills, primary and secondary texts for liberal arts, professional and scholarly journal articles, news archives, and the like.

If you are lucky enough to live in a big city with a well-funded public library, that may be all you need. It will have a large collection of books and journals, and is likely to give you online access to a wider variety of scholarly journals from computers on site. You may be able to print articles or save PDF files to a USB drive.

If you're not near a large public library, here are some good tricks for getting access to the materials you want, and sometimes the buildings that house the books.

Interlibrary Loan (ILL) is a godsend to independent learners. Even the smallest town library is part of the ILL system. Any book you find out about and want to get your hands on can be requested via ILL. Your library will find a copy at another institution and have it sent to their collection temporarily, just for you.

If you live in a town that's home to a college or university, you may be able to use it. Ask at the security or information desk (whichever you can get to) about their policy for community member access. They are often quite generous, ranging from free entry to borrowing privileges. Any state school is likely to have the most open policies. In some states, this is mandated.

If your local college or university library won't let you in, here is my favorite work-around: Check to see if your library or a nearby library houses a Federal Depository Library, sometimes called a Government Documents Center. These are repositories of copies of federal documents (for example, US Senate proceedings). The public is guaranteed access to these documents, and for the most part, they are housed within the main library. So the trick is to go to the security desk and tell them you are there to use the government documents. They will write you a day pass and you walk in the door. You are now free to use the entire building's resources. It won't get you borrowing privileges, but it's a way in. See **Resources**, p. 179.

Evaluate sources of information

Because you'll be depending heavily on sources of information that you find for yourself, it's important to know how to evaluate information for reliability and quality. This has become ever more important since technology has opened the tools of publishing to everyone. Your goal here is to become a savvy consumer of information. There are several keys to this:

- Triangulate your sources, which means reading more than one source for the same information and comparing their approaches and conclusions. For example, if you are learning about the politics of the Middle East, you'll find perspectives from different cultures, different political orientations, and different time periods.
- Probe the background references relied on by the source you're using and learn to assess the context in which the information was produced (including the funding sources, if any). For example, if you are using general media and they report on conclusions of a new scientific study, it's a good idea to track down the original study. Often studies are misrepresented or only part of their conclusions are reported. You will also want to look at the funding sources for the study and the degree to which they may be motivated by business or political concerns.
- Look up the authors of the material, and consider the other things they've written and their biographical details. For example, if you discover that the

author of a book you're reading was in the military in his youth, that will give you some information about the angle from which he perceives the world.

All of this helps you identify biases and track how an original reference is used in service of an argument about facts or how the world works.

Wikipedia is a reasonable place to start, but it's merely an encyclopedia. You wouldn't stop there if it was a physical encyclopedia. What's better about it than a physical encyclopedia is that it is peer edited. This means that anyone who finds incorrect or vague information is able to correct or delete the entry. Looking at the change history and discussion pages for a few Wikipedia entries is itself a great lesson in evaluating information. Citations are supposed to be provided for any information added to a Wikipedia entry. Looking at the sources is also a good idea, both to see if the information appears to be coming from a reliable source, and for some options for further research. In general, Wikipedia is more reliable for scientific information, though it can also be more technical, so it's not always helpful for beginners.

For academic information, finding a "review article" on your subject is a wonderful shortcut for gaining a variety of perspectives and having them identified for you. A review article summarizes and compares a large number of books and studies on a specific topic, such as cognitive science or the work of the philosopher Nietzsche. Review articles are usually published in scholarly journals. If you're not sure how to find them, the reference librarian at your local library can help you.

Stick with it

Getting motivated and sticking with it are actually easier for independent learners than for many classroom students. You're going to be working on something you're passionate or curious about, something you feel strongly that you need to know. You are going to have autonomy over what you're learning and how you're learning it.

Community

The most significant factor in staying motivated and learning effectively is participation in learning communities of any size. A ready-made community is one of the few advantages of formal school, but you've seen in the interviews here that it's also an easy thing to get access to without school. You can track down existing communities of learners, or start your own. One good strategy is to search for email lists related to the subject you're interested in. Additionally, you can ask friends to join you in your learning project or to refer you to other people interested in the same area. Start a reading or skill-learning group for people who want to learn what you're learning or find one. Attend classes or open workspace sessions at a local hackerspace. Ask friends who might know of a group of students working on an extracurricular project and offer to help out. One great independent learning secret is that people I interviewed who liked college usually said that one of the best parts was their extracurricular collaborations—so you can join in on those without paying tuition.

Community is also important to your learning because your community gives you feedback on what you are making and thinking about. Discussion, disagreement, debate, critique, suggestions, corrections, and reinforcement all contribute to making sure you're improving your skills and knowledge. These activities hold you to a community standard of rigorous thought or quality of creative work.

You can use a learning community to give yourself nonarbitrary accountability to the pace of your learning and the depth of your learning. Nonarbitrary means the deadline exists for a consequential reason, usually because it has an effect on others if you don't meet it. For instance, a deadline that's tied to a specific amount of time you have to finish something, like time off from work. In that case, telling other people what you're setting out to accomplish can help hold you to your plans. Another effective deadline strategy is a deadline that is set so that a group can accomplish something together (such as reading a book by a certain date); this is a community responsibility, and it's easier to hold yourself to than a randomly chosen deadline, whether it's from a syllabus or from a personal schedule. Yes, you could read that book next month instead of now, but if your friends are expecting you to lead a discussion on it, you're more likely to do it now, to keep your learning in the present rather than in a hypothetical future. Simply declaring your intentions to others is another way of holding yourself accountable.

Learning within a community is a collective activity. You collaborate, share, teach, and learn. It's important to be a community member who contributes—community is a two-way street. Offering to teach others something you already know is the best way to join or initiate a learning community. You're introducing yourself as a positive contributor as well as an eager learner.

Keeping track of what you learn and internalizing knowledge
Research shows that people who have autonomy over their learning and learn new things in concrete contexts have stronger retention of what they've learned. So you've already got a leg up on this as an independent learner.

Keeping track and internalizing what you learn is another area in which you'll need to explore options and figure out what works best for you. Some people take copious notes, both systematically and unsystematically. They use notebooks, index cards, or programs such as Evernote and Scrivener. Others teach their new skills or knowledge in an informal context. For many people, simply the act of discussing what they've learned in conversation is all they need to make it stick. Writing summaries or reflections about your learning and sharing them with others is also a great strategy, particularly if you are involved in or looking for a community of learners. If you are making a project, you may find that the project itself and the failed attempts by which you've figured out how to make it are a clear and useful record of what you've learned. Some learners collect scraps and make doodles of what they're learning.

Some of the people I spoke with reported that they are not very good at keeping notes or records on what they're learning, but that contextual learning is how they internalize and hold on to what they've learned.

If you're eager to find a written strategy for recording what you've learned, check out the **Resources** section, p. 179, for more information on formal note-taking systems and software for note-taking.

Getting help

Your community is going to be your first stop for getting help when you get stuck or are confused. This could be your in-person community or online communities you're part of, whether it's your social network or a relatively anonymous helping community such as Stack Overflow. Start asking around if you need help; chances are that if nobody knows the answer, at least one person will be able to refer you to someone with the ability to help you. Online help forums for specific skills and areas of knowledge are plentiful, and practicing the ability to find your own answers by asking others and seeing what others have already asked and answered is a skill independent learners develop. These skills are also a significant advantage in the world of work.

You might think that access to professors and experts is an exclusive privilege of being a registered student, but this is far from the truth. Independent learners frequently get in touch with experts who are more than willing to help them or discuss their ideas and knowledge.

You're likely to get a better response if you make sure to clearly express both your enthusiasm for the subject and the fact that you've done some "homework" already. Most of these people are willing to be generous, but they're also busy. Here are some tips for reaching out:

- Read their work or look at their projects before you write to them.
- Ask specific and detailed questions that are relatively brief. Don't ask questions that can be answered by a thorough Google search.
- Give positive feedback; briefly tell them what excites you about their work or the ways in which it has influenced you. If you want to find out about their other work, make sure you've already used the standard tools and give them a sense of the work you know about. If they have a large body of work, it's okay to ask them where you should look next given your particular interests.
- Expect relatively brief responses and only ask follow-on questions if you're invited to.

Get a job

People who haven't done much independent learning tend to be concerned about getting jobs without degrees, whether it's an undergraduate or an advanced degree. Most of the people I spoke with didn't have any problems finding work and keeping jobs. Some of them cited their independent learning as an advantage in the workplace because they have better skills in learning on the job. Here are their job-seeking secrets.

Chutzpah

Getting a job without a degree or required training takes a little bit of chutzpah. You have to be willing to ask an employer to take a risk on you, and to believe in your own competence. Sometimes, you have to be willing to exaggerate your knowledge or skills, knowing by your past experience that you'll know how to learn what you need. This is the idea of "fake it till you make it" that many successful people use to get a foot in the door and learn on the job. It's a strategy that savvy people use, whether they are formally educated or independent learners.

Portfolios

In the absence of the degree that serves as human resources shorthand for being qualified for a job, you'll need to be able to show some work that demonstrates your competence. Work done for previous jobs is great, as are side projects, blogs, any documentation of work you've done or experimented with in the area. Spec work is also a good strategy—make something that's similar to the work you'd be doing at the job you want. If you want work as a graphic designer, mock up an ad design or book cover. Or better yet, find a friend who needs work like that done and trade services with them.

With any portfolio, it's important to explain two things, briefly. The first is what your goal was in making the work you're presenting. The second is how it relates to the job or type of job you're trying to get and the path you took in making it. Your side project may not specifically demonstrate the skills a job requires, but it might show your ability to learn new skills quickly, collaborate with others, and adapt to changing circumstances and needs. Both of these will show your ability to communicate effectively, and that's a huge advantage for any job.

Start small

The idea of starting in an entry-level position, working for a small or growing business or organization, has gotten a little lost in the recent generation that experienced several economic booms. Historically, though, it's a really successful approach for independent learners and the formally educated alike. If your goal is to work for the *New York Times* someday, get a job at your local paper first. If you want to be an entrepreneur, get a job working in a growing business and learn it from the ground up. If you want to be an artist, consider a job as an artist's assistant. These are just a few examples. What's essential is that you approach the job with the attitude of an apprentice. This is your training ground. Find mentors within the organization. Ask good questions and ask them often. Be willing to try new things and take risks in your work. Be as helpful as you can to the people you're learning from.

Tap your learning community

The people you've been learning with will be able to give you leads on jobs, help you figure out the best way to present yourself, give you feedback on your portfolio, provide work references and personal references for job applications, and support you in learning new things you need to know to get a particular job you're excited about. Ask for help and make sure to offer it when other people in your community are in the same boat.

RESOURCES

Resources

Collaborative learning systems

The people I spoke with about independent learning unanimously agreed that learning with others is one of the things they depend on. No one has really solved the challenge of making an ideal online system for collaborative learning. Below are some very interesting attempts that I recommend investigating.

Piazza	piazza.com	Real-time collaborative learning tool for classrooms, adaptable to independent learning groups.
TeamUp	teamup.aalto.fi	A new application for forming groups to learn skills or interests and record progress.
Lore	lore.com	A service designed for educational institutions to run courses, including discussion tools. Adaptable to independent learning groups.
Einztein	einztein.com	Designed for educators and independent learners to form and participate in learning groups.
OpenStudy	openstudy.com	Collaborative platform for open courseware with a nominal fee, offers certificates.

NB	nb.mit.edu/welcome	A tool for annotating online course material that can be shared among groups. It was designed for teachers but can be a great tool for independent learning groups.
/mentoring	mentoring.is	Distributed mentoring site for mentors and mentees to connect.
Social Media Classroom	socialmediaclass room.com	Open source service for groups including integrated forums, blog, comment, wiki, chat, social bookmarking, RSS, microblogging, widgets, and video commenting.

Massive open online course (MOOC) platforms

At the time of this writing, you'll find a dozen free and tuition-based large-scale online courses. The available options and formats are changing rapidly.

Coursera	coursera.org	Currently offers the widest range of subject areas, including sciences and math, technology, liberal arts, and many others.
Udemy	udemy.com	Technology and business classes, including introductions to commonly used office software.
Udacity	udacity.com	Offers primarily science, math, and technology courses.
edX	edx.org	Technology, sciences, math, and expanding to include liberal arts. Anecdotally, I've heard the most positive feedback about edX courses.

Semester Online	semesteronline.org	For credit, tuition-based online courses from a variety of universities, launching in the fall of 2013.
Minerva Project	minervaproject.com	Not yet launched at the time of this writing, Minerva Project is a tuition-based program.
Academic Earth	academicearth.org	Courses in the form of video lectures in a variety of subjects from top universities.
P2PU	p2pu.org	A platform for anyone to organize a course and form groups to collaborate, complete assignments, and give feedback.
University of the People	uopeople.org	Tuition-free online university, with nominal processing fees. Not yet accredited.
Alison	alison.com	Free courses and programs primarily oriented around job training, offering certificates.
The Open University	open.ac.uk	The Open University has been offering distance learning since 1969, and continues to be an excellent place to learn online.

Other forms of free and low-cost online learning

Codeacademy	codeacademy.com	Codeacademy is a free, lesson-based way to learn programming.
Skillcrush	skillcrush.com	Skillcrush is another free programming education site.
Treehouse	teamtreehouse.com	Treehouse is a free resource for "job-ready" tech education.

Google Developers University Consortium	developers.google.com/university	University Consortium has a variety of courses in programming for more advanced coders.
Dorkbot	dorkbot.org	Local chapters of Dorkbot—community showcases and email lists of technologists, tinkerers, artists, and geeks.
DIY MFA	diymfa.com	DIY MFA is an alternative to a formal master in fine arts for writers, founded by an MFA grad.
Faux MBA	fauxmba.com/book-list	The Faux MBA's reading list can be found here.
Open-CourseWare	opencontent.org/ocwfinder & ocwconsortium.org	OpenCourseWare is offered by many universities, with free course syllabi and audio or video lectures.
BBC *Languages*	bbc.co.uk/languages	The BBC hosts a language-learning site. It is not currently being updated but remains useful.

If you are interested in learning a particular coding language (such as Arduino, Ruby, Python, and a host of others), go to the website for that coding language to find tutorials and in-depth learning materials.

In general, YouTube hosts endless how-to videos, from ballroom dancing to technology projects. They vary in quality, but can be a useful addition to your learning toolbox.

Local learning

There are a number of new organizations that allow people to teach what they know and for learners to find what they need, either for free or at very low cost. They tend to be local and in-person, although they're expanding and evolving at a very fast rate. If these models appeal to you, get in touch with the founders and find out about starting an outpost in your city.

Skillshare	skillshare.com	Skillshare is a platform for anyone to teach what they know.
Trade School	tradeschool.coop	Trade School is a learning barter platform.
L'Ecole Des Beaux Arts	ldbabrooklyn.com/ xoxo/classes	L'Ecole Des Beaux Arts offers artistic and skill-based classes taught by artists and tradespeople.
Hackerspaces	hackerspaces.org/ wiki	For technical skills and shared tools from hammers to laser cutters, hackerspaces are a fantastic resource. They're collectives for people who share skills, knowledge, and equipment. Some are members-only, but most have at least an occasional evening that's open to the public.

Textbooks and curricula

Less Wrong	lesswrong.com	Less Wrong is a community of people investigating rationality and cognition. The site includes a great list of best textbooks.
Ask MetaFilter	ask.metafilter.com	Ask MetaFilter is a good source for textbooks and curricula, with many suggestions and explanations of why particular books are better or worse.
Open- CourseWare	opencontent.org/ ocwfinder & ocwconsortium.org	Mentioned above, OpenCourseWare, in addition to offering video lectures, is a good place to start if you're just looking for syllabi and other open course materials.

Connexions	cnx.org	Connexions is a free educational material repository.

Access to scholarly publishing

Directory of Open Access Journals	doaj.org	See the Directory of Open Access Journals in scholarly publishing.
Directory of Open Access Books	doabooks.org	Directory of peer-reviewed Open Access academic books.
Knowledge Unlatched	knowledge unlatched.org	Knowledge Unlatched is a way to publish and access open scholarly books.

In addition, many major journal publishers have at least a few open access journals, so a search of "open access journals" will provide new material as well.

Google Scholar	scholar.google.com	Google Scholar searches only scholarly publications, rather than the web in general.
Abstract Science	is.gd/itizos	As always, when working with academic materials, it's important to have evaluation skills. Noah Gray of the Huffington Post wrote an extremely useful guide to understanding the short abstracts at the beginning of scientific papers.
Learning Historical Research	is.gd/osoqur	Historian William Cronon (a personal favorite of mine) offers a how-to site, Learning Historical Research. It's an in-depth resource on how to do academic scholarly research.

Access to library materials

There are two ways to get access to library materials that your local free library doesn't have.

Find the books you want by searching university or public library databases. Write down the information and take it to the reference desk at your public library. Tell the librarian you'd like to order the book through Interlibrary Loan.

There's also a way to get into many university libraries that aren't open to the public. If the central library houses a Federal Depository Library, it is mandatory that the public have access to it. So, walk in and tell the security desk you're there to use the Depository or Government Documents Center, as it is sometimes called. That's it. You're in.

You can find a complete list of **Federal Depository Libraries** at is.gd/afeyeq, then click the FDLP Public page link.

Note-taking systems

Few of the people I interviewed used formal note-taking systems, though some used online or smartphone programs.

The Top 12 Note Taking Apps	is.gd/hikibi	Lifehack offers a list of favorite programs.
Fetchnotes	fetchnotes.com	Fetchnotes is a recently launched note-taking program created by undergraduate students from the University of Michigan.
Note Taking Systems	is.gd/bazofu	The Academic Skills Center at Cal Poly in San Luis Obispo has a detailed guide to formal written note-taking systems.

Questions and answers

Getting questions answered online is easy. And the great part is that almost always, someone else has already asked your question and had it answered.

The hard part is learning to evaluate the sources of the information you find. See the **Evaluate Sources of Information** section, p. 177.

Some go-to sources for getting answers are:

Khan Academy	khanacademy.org	Khan Academy has short, quality tutorials in a wide variety of subjects.
MetaFilter Ask MetaFilter	metafilter.com & ask.metafilter.com	MetaFilter and Ask MetaFilter are endlessly useful sources of answers to questions. If your question hasn't already been asked, you'll have to join the community, with a nominal fee, to ask.
Stack Overflow	stackoverflow.com	For programmers, Stack Overflow is a rich resource where coders ask questions and share code.
Wolfram Alpha	wolframalpha.com	Wolfram Alpha has extensive resources for math- and science-related questions.

It goes without saying that searching Google is very useful. You can type in your question, and chances are you'll find an answer. Many answers. But, this is where your evaluation skills will come in handy. As you search a lot, you'll also get better at framing questions that are specific enough to lead to useful answers more quickly.

Wikipedia is wonderful, but also requires evaluation skills. Anyone can make a page, and anyone can edit it. If someone adds information or changes it, they are required by convention to cite their sources. When sources are consistently absent, the page will usually be flagged as unreliable or needing verification. Scientific and scholarly information is overall fairly reliable. In any case, learn how to understand where the information in a Wikipedia article is coming from. It's a good place to start, but it's never a good place to end your research.

A selection of further readings

Don't Go Back to School is an ethnographic project, which means it is drawn first from observing and gathering first-person reports on the subject. It's important not to let other people's theories and research color what you ask and what you hear from your subjects. Beyond what I already knew from prior reading, I limited my explorations of theories of learning and movements for reform until after the interviews were done.

Research about adult learning outside of school can be found mostly in the vast literature on adult vocational education. Within that literature, the work of Malcolm Knowles stands out.

For this project, some of the most inspiring books about learning outside of school and changing classroom education actually focus on grade school and high school classrooms, and none of them are new. For years, these writers have inspired and informed homeschooling. The most significant include:

Ivan Illich's 1971 book *Deschooling Society* can be read online here: is.gd/ejobok.

Grace Llewellyn's *Teenage Liberation Handbook: How to Quit School and Get a Real Life and Education* is a classic, first published in 1991.

John Holt's work, beginning in the 1960s, has been influential to proponents and practitioners of alternative education. A list of his books, with excerpts from each can be found here: is.gd/itidiv.

More recently, Tony Wagner's work on teaching innovation for children and teenagers mirrors some of what I've found related to adults: tonywagner. com/tag/books.

Teaching practices for "project-based learning" in K–12 are a useful resource both for teachers and for adults interested in collaborative learning: is.gd/ripako.

Beyond the world of K–12 education reform a few sources informed my post-interview thinking.

Edward L. Deci's scholarly work on motivation has been influential in confirming the material in my interviews related to motivation. He has also written a general-audience book called *Why We Do What We Do*.

Theories and practices of constructivist learning, based on a long history of psychological ideas about how people learn, have been useful in my post-interview research and often echo the conclusions I reached. A useful overview can be found here: is.gd/eloduz.

Jean Lave and Etienne Wenger's *Situated Learning* (1991) focuses on learning as an act that takes place in context rather than a transfer of knowledge in the abstract, closely mirroring the experiences of my interviewees.

I've been following changes in the engineering and physics departments at MIT, which have been developing classroom practices and configurations that provide learning environments designed with forms of independent learning in mind. Their innovations are an exciting step toward reform within the system.

For an extensive list of links to the resources and research I've collected on education, learning, student debt, and other topics related to this book, see: is.gd/kihodo.

—

Seth Godin's *Stop Stealing Dreams (What Is School For?)*, is an impassioned, provocative manifesto written to provoke teachers to change their classroom practices in ways that reflect the findings of *Don't Go Back to School*. Godin includes an excellent bibliography for teachers: is.gd/monuru.

The brand-new *Peeragogy Handbook* is another useful resource on peer learning for classroom innovators and anyone who wants to form a peer-learning group. It is based on extensive academic research and contains a multitude of references to theories of peer learning as well as practical guidance: peeragogy.org.

For current scholarly resources on free learning and learning technologies, see Pepperdine University doctoral student Rolin Moe's public bibliography of the scholarly resources underlying his work: is.gd/bedadi.

Thiel Fellow Dale J. Stephens' *Hacking Your Education: Ditch the Lectures, Save Tens of Thousands, and Learn More Than Your Peers Ever Will* (2012) offers current advice on succeeding in careers without a degree.

Education journalist (and serial dropout) Audrey Watters' Hack Education site is a fantastic resource for new developments and savvy commentary: hackeducation.com.

Anya Kamenetz's reporting for *Fast Company* tracks the economics of higher education and advocates for learner-centric higher education reform. She's also the author of two useful books on the topic, DIY U (2010) and *Generation Debt* (2006): is.gd/ididij.

Acknowledgments

Above all else, I could not have made this book without Kickstarter, the 1,588 people who backed the project and cheered me on, and the 90 people who talked with me about how they learn. The names of my interviewees and backers are listed in the pages that follow.

There is no more powerful lever than the insistent encouragement and loving support of my partner Bre Pettis, who was also instrumental in getting the book started and getting it done. My mother's role as a devoted grandmother gave me the time to do it.

I'm grateful to Richard Nash, Karen Barbarossa, Clay Shirky, Sherri Wasserman, Juliette Guilbert, Liz Danzico, Dan Sinker, Kim Robinson, Tim Maly, Joshua Glenn, Jodi Baker, Brian McFarland, Doug Rushkoff, and Debbie Chachra, for conversations, feedback, and generosity in sharing knowledge. Members of the HC shared their stories and ideas with me.

Behind the scenes, Familiar Studio's Ian Crowther made this beautiful. Mandy Brown was indispensable as an editor, and Krista Stevens hunted for mistakes. Lori Lawton transcribed the interviews. I thank all of them for their labors.

I wrote most of this at a sunny table in the corner of Nunu Chocolates in Brooklyn. Everyone there cheered me on—in particular Andy, Justine, Josh, and Lydia—with coffee, enthusiasm, and occasional bits of broken chocolate.

Interviewees

Adam Greenfield
Addie Wagenknecht
Alan D. Thompson
Alberic Paradiso
Alec Resnick
Alex Handy
Anindita Basu Sempere
Anonymous
Anonymous
Astra Taylor
Aurelius Prochaska
Barbara Meinel
Bartram Nelson
Benjamen Walker
Brad Edmondson
Brian LaRossa
Cameron Clark
Cameron Rogers
Carla Kaiser
Cate Duffy
Caterina Rindi
Charles Phillips
Chris Bathgate
Chuck Kinnane
Claire Bangser
Cory Doctorow
Cory Ward
Dan Sinker
Dana Rosen
Daniel Byler
Daniel Thorne
Danny Iny
David Hirmes
David Mason
Devin Rhode

Dorian Taylor
Eliot Lash
Emily Daniels
Eric Ose
Esther Finney
Evangeline Moen
Florian Wagner
Furrygirl
Gene Wolf
Gina Queen
Harper Reed
Henry Wischusen
Jason James
Jenny Davidson
Jeremy Cohen
Jim Munroe
Jimmie P. Rodgers
Joan Ball
John Unger
Josh Sager
Karen Barbarossa
Kayleen Yiltalo-Horsma
Keith Crusher
Ken Baumann
Kevin David Crowe
Kurt Vega
Lana Zellner
Larry Hite
Lenore Edman
Luke Muehlhauser
Michael Busby
Molly Crabapple
Molly Danielsson
Nathan Frund
Nicholas Tozier

Nick Bogdanoff
Nöel Hamer
Pablos Holman
Peter Baumbach
Peter Varshavsky
Quinn Norton
Randy J. Hunt
Rita J. King
Ryan Reif
Sahan Pitigala
Sarah Jasmon
Sarah Laine Milner
Sascha D'Angeli
Simone Davalos
Sonja Landis
Stacie Humpherys
Steffan Antonas
Stephen Lovell
Steve R.
Sufey Chen
Susan Kapuscinski
  Gaylord
Tara Brown
Tarmo Toikkanen
Thomas Winningham
Timi Gleason
Tony Hsieh
Tristan Davies
Tristan Price
Valerie Vande Panne
Witold Riedel
Zack Booth Simpson

Funders

Don't Go Back to School was generously funded by 1,588 individuals, couples, and organizations using Kickstarter. To learn more, visit kck.st/ryAqDU.

"AZ" Zinsious
@sourishkrout
404WHYLO
A Cranstoun
A. Hake
A. Lewellen
A.C. Tang
Aaron "Always Learning" Klenke
Aaron Garrett
Aaron Harmon
Aaron Katz
Aaron Rutledge
Aaron Watkins
Abe Cajudo
Abie Hadjitarkhani
Ada Nzeribe
Adam Allen Anderson
Adam Brault
Adam Brown
Adam Buckheit
Adam Haas
Adam J. Saint
Adam McCall
Adam Parrish
Adam Reger
Adam Tannir
Adnan Arif
Adriane Horovitz
Adrienne Crew
Aitor García Rey
Akiba
Akihiro Tanimura

Al Billings
Al Wasco
Alan Smithee
Alan Teelander
Albert Tong
Albert Varma
Albion L. Gould
Alec McCrindle
Alejandro Knopf
Aleksander R. Nordgarden-Rødner
Alex Chang
Alex Cheek
Alex Crittenden
Alex Hoekstra
Alex Johnston M.Ed.
Alex Nastetsky
Alex Neving
Alexander Grgurich
Alexander Jahn
Alexander Oster
Alexander Weston Bennett
Alexis Hope
alf3
Alia Thabit
Alice Lyu
Alison Quinn
Alister Blake
Allison Fink
Allison G. Meade
Allison Hines
Allison Lyzenga

Alvaro Vargas
Alvin Jackson "Rocky J"
Alyse Liebovich
Amanda Moore
Amar
Amar Baber Ellahi
Amber Landgraff
Amos Brown
Amy Fox
Amy Torgeson
Amy YILDIZLI
Amyas David Gilbert
Anaïs Mathers
Anantharaman
"Anand" Ganesh
Anastasia Vesperman
Andpat
Andras Huszar
Andre Behrens
Andrea Huntley
Andrea La Rose
Andrea Lenhart
Andrea Mignolo
Andrew & Anindita Sempere
Andrew Courter
Andrew Crisp
Andrew K. Butcher
Andrew Krause
Andrew Mostajo Magpoc
Andrew Newton
Andrew Peth
Andrew S

Andrew Styer
Andrew Waddell
Andrew Watson
Andrew White
Andrey Sluzhivoy
Andries De Vos
Angie Kalea Ho
Anil Dash
Ankit Bhargava
Ann Chen
Ann K. Hubbard
anna
Anna Creadick
Annalisa Barrie
Anne Jonas
Annemarie Gray
Anthony Hay
Anthony Watts
Anu M
April Walters
Aram Bartholl
Aris Lambrianidis
Arne Kreutzmann
Art Palmer
Art Sederquist
Ash Chapman
Ash Thames
Ashley Alexander
Ashley Kanak
AshleyRose Butler
Audrey Auden
Audrey Watters
Aura Castro López

Aurelien Gouny

Aurora Björnsdóttir

Aurora Thornhill

Austin J. Austin

Austin Kleon

Avital Oliver

Axel Clarke

ayesha Abbasi

Azmir Saliefendic

Azucena Gee

B. Tse

Balthazar Simões

Barbara Watkins

Barney Debnam

Baxter Stapleton

Bean Snowboards

Bedirhan Cinar

Belal Breaga Bakht

Belea Simion

Belinda S. Chambers

Belle McQuattie

Ben Kilgust

Ben Lainhart

Ben Tseitlin

Benjamin Ortiz

Benjamin Williams

Benjamin Wilson

Bernd Out

Bernhard "Berny" Marx

Beth Pratt

Betty Nikia

Bill Harwood

Bill Stewart

Billimarie Robinson

Billy Shih

Birte Petersen

Blake Boles

Bob Ippolito

Boon Sheridan

Bosco Hernàndez

Brad Barrish

Brad Edmondson &
  Tania Werbizky

Brad Kik

Brad Morris

Brad Oakley

Bradley Bacon

Brady Forrest-Ignite Talks!

Brandon J. Barba

Brandon Milholland

Brandon Walowitz

Bre Pettis

Breck Sargent

Brendan Crain

Brendan Mathews

Brendan Stromberger

Brett Bretterson

Brett Wilson

BREZTECH.NET

Brian Christie

Brian Del Vecchio

Brian Eoff

Brian J. Peterson

Brian P. Frank

Brian Roberts

Brian Wanless

Brodie Rich

Bronwyn Mahoney

Bruce (Peter) Atkinson

Bruce Heroux

Bruce Murray

Bruno Torres

Bry Ashman

Bryan Laroche

Bryan Taketa

Bryan Thatcher

Bryce Anderson

C Schwoerer

c. g. menssen

C. R. Johnson

C'Ella Clayton

Caitlin J Jung

Callan Lamb

Candie Patterson

Candra Murphy

Captain Crunch

Captain Sasha

Carl Hutchison

Carl Williamson

Carla D. Martin

Carla Diana

Carlos

Carmen Hernandez

Carol Gunby

Carol Wagner

Caroline Craffigan

Caroline Rennie

Carter Bancroft

Carynne Miller Corvaia

Case Larsen

Casey Girard

Caterina Fake

Caterina Rindi

Catherine Mikkelsen

Cathy Stern

Cesare Pagura

Chad Ruble

chad...

Charles Daniels

Charles Kinnane

Charles Lim

Charles Magnuson

Charles Wood

Charlie Wang

Cheryl Furjanic

Chetna Patel

Chip Clofine

Chloe S Jones

Chris Alden

Chris Annand

Chris Bathgate

Chris Bushick

Chris Cee

Chris Curran

Chris Currie

Chris Hopp

Chris Hunter

Chris Janes

Chris Kubica

Chris Lee

Chris Maguire

Chris Moyer

Chris Raab

Chris Reynolds

Chris Sullivan

Chris Varner

Chris XM

Christal cody

Christian "DisOrd3r"
  Johansson

Christian H. Gmelin

Christian Hadidjaja

Christian Hudon

Christina Xu

Christine Fluor

Christine P. Fojas

Christophe MOUCHEL

Christopher Angus

Christopher B Phelps

Christopher Benner

Christopher Bodel

Christopher Cao

Christopher Corneschi
Christopher E. Lard
Christopher Gray
Christopher J. Agius
Christopher Mullins
  Warnock
christopher starr
Christopher Varano
Christopher Wright
Christopher Yetter
Chuck & Claudia Pettis
Chuck Corbett
Chuck Petras
Chuck Smith
Claire Oliphant
Clay Shirky
Clay Wiedemann
Cliff J. Grant
Clyde Boyer
coffeehaus
Colin Faulkingham
Colin Keizer
Colin McSwiggen
Colin Shaffer
Colin Zwiebel
Coll Wise
Colleen Benson
Conrad Feagin
Corey Clingo
Corey Van Meekeren
Corey Ward
Cornelius Caesar Gloria
Cory Robinson
Courtney Boyd Myers
Craig Blaylock
Creatrix Tiara
CW&T
Cynthia Lawson Jaramillo

Cynthia Nearman
D Rasmussen
D. James
D.A. Cox
D.A. Gutierrez
Dakin R. Tapp
Dan Carlson
Dan Chambers
Dan Coates
Dan Colomb
Dan Lowe
Dan O'Sullivan
Dan Phiffer
Dan Picton
Dan Rezykowski
Dan Sinker
Dane Bettis
Dane Dormio
Dani Vasquez
Daniel Ahrendt
Daniel C Young
Daniel Compton
Daniel Crowell
Daniel Dingeldey
Daniel Dunnam
Daniel Gill
Daniel J. Johnson
Daniel Lemire
Daniel Magriso
Daniel Nephin
Daniel Read
Daniel Samarin
Daniel Sensenbach
Daniel T Smith
Daniel Tabar
Danielle Burhop
Danielle Rose Stack Jacobs
Danny Iny

Danny J Gros
Danny Pettry II
Daryn Nakhuda
Dave Hinman
Dave LeCompte
Dave Pritchard
Dave Wallingford
David Boyer
David Cooper
David Delony
David Hunter
David J Williamson
David Kessler
David Kramer
David Lee
David Lee-Olmstead
David Liu Lau
David Lu
David M. Minger
David Marcantonio
David Mason
David McMullin
David McRaney
David Murray
David Novosel
David Nuñez
David P Lachs
David Pak
David Papini
David R Wilson
David Recor
David Rioux
David Schleifer
David Vogeleer
David W Yarbrough
David Wilkey
David William Breyer
David Wolske

Dawne Charters-Nelson
Deb Saunders
Debbie Weil
Debra A. Joyner
Declan Kehoe
Declan McGrath
Dennis Chan
Dennis Charles
Dennis J Jacobs
Derek Choi
Derek Rodger
Derrick Bohlin
Devin Fraze
Dewey Manhood
Diana M Woody
Diane Gilleland
Dianna Goodwin
Diego Salazar
Diogo Tolezano
Domingo Remigio
Dominic Jarvis
Dominique Ahkong
don clay
Donna Wallstin
Doug Leedham
Dox Doxiadis
Dr Toby James Andrews
Dr. Alysia Fischer
Dr. Beverly Yuen
  Thompson
Dr. Chrystal Denmark
  Porter
Dragos Ionel
Drew Petersen
Duncan Dodd
Dustin Woodard
Dustyn Roberts
Dylan Steer

Dylan Zacherle
E. Allred
E. Cagmat
E. Guerrero
E. Wiens
E.K. Weaver
Eamae Mirkin
Ed Sherman
Ed White
Eddy E Farhat
Eileen Can
Elena Murphy
Eleni Thanou
Eliot Graythorne
Eliot Lash
Elisabeth Robson
Elizabeth Eyerer
Elizabeth Harshaw
Ellen Zemlin
Elliot Eubanks
Ellis Reilly
Elroy Davis
Emeka Okafor
Emerald Levick
Emily C
Emily Daniels
Emily Leuning
Emma Davies
Eric Andrade
Eric Beland
Eric Corl
Eric Goff
Eric Krupa
Eric Meltzer
Eric Nakagawa
Eric Ose
Eric Rucker
Eric Skiff

Erin McElhinney
Ernesto J. Torres
Espen Steinsnes
Esther Egerton
Eugene & Vonnie Chan
Eugene Meidinger
Evan Cordes
Evan Morrison
Ewan Adams
Fabio Sarabia
Fatos Gjakova
Felipe Madrigal
Felix Faassen
Fernando Blat
FILMSTORY.ORG
fin
Florian Wagner
Floris Vermeir
Francesca Verdier
Frank Chimero
Franklin Wallbrown
Franz-Philipp Schmuker
Frederic Levesque
FurryGirl
G.
G. Scott Morris
Gœtz S.
Gabriel Beaudoin
Gabriel Ochoa
Gabriel Rosas
Gail Whiffen
Galen Mancino
Gannon Beck
Garrett Belmont
Gary Chong
Gary Parsons
Geek & Dad, LLC
Gene Becker

Gene Zhou
Genevieve Gorta
Genya Turovskaya
Geoff Allemand (iLearn
   in the REAL world)
Geoff Urland
Geoffrey Bonser
George Arriola
George Ramos
Gerard Ramos
Gerhard Lindeque
Gert
Girish Arora
Golan Levin
Grace Antonas
Grady Wright
Graeme Asher
Grandpa
Grant Benson
Greg Borenstein
Greg Cooksey
Greg McDougall
Greg Robinson
Greg Roth
Gregory Hirsch
Gregory Miller
Gregory Stromberg
Griff Maloney
Guillermo Martinez
Gus Rojo
Gus Zantanon
Gustavo Barron (Cicloid)
Guy Vardi
Gwen Bell
H Lynnea Johnson
Hadassah S. Hickman
Håkon Knappskog
Hal Gottfried

Hannah Eason
Hannah Margolin
Hannah O'Kane
Har Rai
Hartley Brody
Hasan Gopalani
Heath Holmes
Heather Burrell
Heather Walker
Heather Wilson
Helen Michaud
Helen Walters
Helen Y.
Helmut
Henry McKenzie
Henry Wischusen
High Cove
Highland Dryside
   Rusnovs
Holly Green
Hollyrinny
HowTutorial.com
Hugh Reynolds
Hugo
Hugo Mesquita
Ian Crowther
Ilse Godts
India Amos
Indigo King
Irwin FV
Isaac Watson Stephenson
Ishaque Hussain
Ivo Beckers
J Reek
J Tuente
J. E. Yochim
J. M. Lee
J. Rothweiler

J.Campbell

J.D. Hollis

Jack Conroy

Jack Kerns

Jack Maus

Jack Price

Jackson Tsai

Jacky Tang

Jacob Attrill

Jacob Kravetz

Jacques Ecuyer

jae maddox

Jaime Joel Jimenez

Jairo A. Marin

Jakob Schnaidt

James Anthony

James Floyd Kelly

James Trotter

Jamison Schweitzer

Jan Beilicke

Jan Michael Maluto

Jan Vantomme

Janelle Ward

Janien Fadich

Janna Jude Brown

Jared Congiardo

Jared Nielsen

Jarrod Pirtle

Jason

Jason Daugherty

Jason Dyer

Jason Li

Jason Naumoff

Jason R Turner

Jason R. Mosack

Jason Rugolo

Jason Scott

Jaswant

Javier Ordóñez

Jay "Null Flow" Kim

Jay Buerck

Jay C

Jay Liu

Jaymee Mak

JD Scott

Jeanette Inthisorn

Jeanine Melanson

Jeannie Voirin-Gerde

Jed

Jed Lingat

Jef W.

Jeff 'foxxtrot' Craig

Jeff Sapp

Jeffery Ugbah

Jeffrey Eran

Jeffrey Willis

Jen Chau

Jen Weintraub

Jennifer & Nowell
    Creadick

Jennifer Leonard

Jennifer Marcson

Jennifer Mathis

Jennifer Skahen

Jennifer Sweeney

Jennifer Walker

Jenny Lawton

Jeremiah Johnson

Jeremiah Lee

Jeremy Hulette

Jeremy Leung

Jeremy Quinn

Jeremy Sprague

Jeremy Wadhams

Jerry Huey

Jerry Isdale

Jerry Proctor

Jeshii

Jesse Fisher

Jesse M Howatt

Jesse Moore

Jesse Russell

Jessica Frances Braz

Jessica Hammer

Jessica Johnson

Jessica Yogini

Jessie Brodsky

Jigesh Mehta

Jillian Brooks

Jim Pfeiffer

Jim Takahashi

Jimmy LaRue

Jince Kuruvilla

JiraJ

JJ Casas

Joan Cabaddu

Joanne McNeil

João Valente

Jodi Baker

Jodi Colella

jodi morrison

Joe Hughes

Joe Santa Cruz

Joel

Joel Hough

John "papa" Cotter

John Bowditch

John Colagioia

John Devor

John Dimatos

John Hergenroeder

John Hodge

John Hupp

John Ibarzabal

John J. Rynne

John L. Kingery

John L. Olson

John M Stein

John McCarthy

John McVey

John Mooney

John R. Dougan

John Rogers

john schroder

John Semeleer

John T. Unger

John Tollefsen

Joi & Jared Kruger

Jolanda

Jon Crispin

Jon Haufe

Jon Osborne

Jon Siddle

Jon W. Zeitler

Jonathan Ferrer Custodio

Jonathan Fusellier

Jonathan Klick

Jonathan Liss

Jonathan McManus

Jonathan Unikowski

Jonny Lee

Jordan Budisantoso

Jordan Bunker

Jordan Lee Knape

Jordan Rosner

Jorge Lugo

Jose da Costa

Joseph Keenan

Josh Catone

Josh Hartung

Josh Swihart

Joshua Beale

joshua fouts

Joshua Glenn

Joshua James

Joshua Keesee

Joshua Loy

Joshua Lutz

Joshua Madara

Joshua Sager

Joshua Stylman

Joshua Vergara

Josselin Perrus

JP Rangaswami

Juana Olga Barrios

Julia Fariss

Julia Richards

Julia Wilson

Julian Gates

Juliet Blake

Justin B. Thompson

Justin Charles

Justin Day

Justin J.M. Campoli

Justin M Owens

Justin Ritchie

Justin Smith

Justin Trimm

Jyri Engeström

K. Knapp

Kabron Bingham

Kacie Kinzer

Kai Hawk

Kalee Featherwise

Kamil Sliwowski

Karen Clark

KAREN F MAYER

Karen Feng

Karen Rustad

Karey Pohn, JD, PhD

Kari Sullivan

Karine Ardault

Karl Sakas

Karol Gajda

Kat Ethington

Kate Hartman

Kate Knight

Kate Knolls

Katha Trænkle

Katherine Davis

Katherine Lawrence

Kathleen McGivney

Kathy E. Wright

Kathy T

Katie Turner

Kato Murray

Katy Watkins

Kaydee Kreitlow

Kayla Daniels

Kelley E. Anderson

Kelly A. Spoer

Kelly Blades

Kelly Stegall

Kelly Webster

Ken Baumann

Ken Goddard

Ken Mickles

Ken T.

kendel ratley

Kendra Wiig

Keri Korteling

Kerri Miller

Kevin A. & Tina O. Shaw

Kevin Connolly

Kevin J. Diedrick

Kevin Lewis

Kevin Loney

Kevin Neufeld

Kevin O. Lepard

Kevin Walker

Kiddy Prisons

Kim & Will Honeycutt

Kim Robinson

Kimberley Peter

Kirk S.

Kirsten Lyons

Kirsty Win

Kitt Hodsden

Kiyoshi

Koert Schonewille

Kris Budhu

Kris Gale

Kristelle Aisaka

Kristina Garrels

Kristina Lee

Kristof Lemp

Kyla Ryman

Kyle Bylin

Kyle Largent

Kyle medeyum garlock

Kyle O'Brien

L. A. Miller

Larry & Tona Hattery

Larry Lo

Larry Mason

Lars Harder

Lash LaRue

Laszlo Kiss

Laura Bazzetta

Laura Bilazarian

Laura Galloway

Laura Greig

Laura Jansen

Laura Kanzler

Laura Wolf-Powers

Lauren A. Pitts

Lauren Gardner

Lauren Probert

Laurie Adams

Laurie Glatt

Laurie Monday
Timberlake

Lea Tui

Leah Lubman

Lee Aylward

Lee-kai Wang

Leen van Dalen

Leila Anasazi

Lertad Supadhiloke

Less Antman

Lester Koh

Leticia Britos Cavagnaro

Lezlie Amara Piper

Liangjie Xia

Lidor Brosh

Liesje Hodgson

Lim Tee Lip

Linda Ballantine

Linda Edeiken in
honor of Joe

Lindsay Bernath

Linette True

Lisa

Lisa Kovacevich

Lisandro Gaertner

Liz Danzico

Liz Tomazic

Lizanne Witte

Lola Mullen

Lorenzo Orselli

Lorenzo Santos

Lori Christopher

Lorie A. Johnson

Lorien Green

Lotus M Jones

Lou Ronnau

Luane Todd

Lucia Jeesun Lee

Lucy Rudenborg

Luis Miguel Hervella

Luis-José Torres

Luke Brooks

Luke Kastelic

Luke Leonard

Lydia Pettis

Lynn Cook

LynneFarrow.net

M. Huynh

M. Lisa Phipps

M. Stewart

Magali Value

Mangala Branka Tokic

ManMeetsStove.com

Manny Flores

Mara Zepeda |

Switchboard

Marcello Seri

Marci Turpin

Marcis Curtis

Marcus Denker

Maria C. Fadda

Maria Mercedes Martinez

Mariana de Carvalho

Rodrigues

Marina Gijzen

Mario Warren

Marjori Pomarole

Mark Atwood

Mark Fonseca Rendeiro

Mark Glitch

Mark Graham Dunn

Mark K. - Cape Town

Mark Kingwell

Mark LaRocca

Mark Milotay

Mark Movic

Mark Russell

Mark Sessoms

Mark Sturgell,

pdncoach.com

Mark. Alder

Markus Laumann

Marta Soncodi

Martin Flueler

Martin Storbeck

(@hdready)

Marty Day

Marty McGuire

Mary Anne Shew

Mary Buhr

Mary Catherine Cusack

Mary Elisabeth Barbour

Mary Frances Barzee

Mary Nichols (DJ Fu-

sion/FuseBox Radio

Broadcast)

Mary Rock

mashehu

Mason Mindanao

Mat S.

Mathieu Gauthier

Mathieu Gingras

Mathieu Tourneur

Matt Blain

Matt Butson

Matt D

Matt Duhamel

Matt Grommes

Matt Perkins

Matt Royal

Matt Soell

Matt Warshaw

Matthew Cranor

Matthew Eichmann

Matthew Feifarek

Matthew Griffin

Matthew H.

Matthew J McLaughlin

Matthew Knowles

Matthew Leone

Matthew Mark Kroeger

Matthew Sauter

Matthew Wheeland

Matthias Ludwig

Maurice Gaston

Mauricio Cordero

Mauricio Espinosa de

los Monteros

Max Fenton

Mayim Stapleton

Meaghan B. Whalen

Meg Withgott

Megan Hustad

Megan Marz

Meimei Fong

Meister Bananengrips

Melissa Bee Farm &

Aquaponic Gardens

Melodie Woods

Merve Karasu

Meryl Stark

Mia Eaton

Michael Baldwin

Michael Bennett Cohn

Michael C Lawyer

Michael Chanter

Michael Declerck

Michael E. Duffy

Michael Kane

Michael Leibel

Michael Markowitz

Michael Mattox

Michael Meigs-

McDonald

Michael Pagano

Michael Paterson

Michael Rasmussen/

MichaelRpdx

Michael Underwood

Michael Zeltner

Michelle Donahoe

Michelle Dunn

Michelle Myers

Miguel Marcos

Mikael

Mike Barraclough

mike boon.

Mike Cardarelli

Mike Cullen

Mike Dory

Mike Farmer

Mike Haeg

Mike Paunovich

Mike Terry

Mike Vanderipe

mikeho

Miles Lightwood

Millie Hayes

Mindy Tchieu

Ming Hwa Ting

MiriamintheMidwest

Mirza Rahman

Misha Hoekstra

Mister Carlisle

Misty Harper

Mitchell Rasor

MK Mercurio
Moe McIntyre
Mogens
Molly Ho
Molly Steenson
Mona T Morgan
Monika Smyczek
Morgan Woroner
Moriah Simmons
mosse
Mr & Mrs N Clarke
Mr. Bucky Fukumoto
MW Malcolm
Mystic Murray
N. D. Pruitt
Nancy Daniels
Nancy Seubert
Nassim Wahba
Natalia Ziolkowski
Nathan Black
Nathan Griffith
Nathaniel Griggs
Neil Freeman
Nicco Wargon
Nicholas Contino
Nick Dalton
Nick Hoath
Nick Nielsen
Nick Nieman
Nick Parish
Nick Turner
Nicky Wolveri Hajal
Nicola Twilley
Nicolas Salerno
Nicole Hennig
Nicole Jones
Niesha B
Nikolai Warner

Nina Ribbeklint
Nishan Karassik
Noah Iliinsky
Nora Abousteit
Nortd Labs
North Pacific Company
Nysa Wong Kline
Oliver Janoschka
Oliver Pospisil
Olivier Mével
Onno Hoogendoorn
Ope Bukola
Ophir Ronen
Oscar
Oscar Von Hauske
Owen Wesley Kerschner
Pablos
Pamela Day
Pat McGarry
Pat Santilli
Patrick Corwin
Patrick Grogan
Patrick M. Lozeau
Patrick Neil
patrick phelan
Patrick Tanguay
Paul A. Wilson, PhD
Paul Bennetts
Paul H. Hyman
Paul Kaiser
Paul M Ramos
Paul M. Wirsing
Paul McGrath
Paul Reynolds
Paul Rothrock
Paul Staunton
Paul Taylor
Paul Tildesley

Pawel
Pedro Silva
Penny Nickle
Perica Cesko
Pete "Patch" Alberti
Pete Welter
Peter A. Johnson
Peter Boardman
Peter DuMont
Peter G. Haendler
PETER MANSFIELD
Peter McQuillan
Peter Purgathofer
Peter S Maylott
Peter T. Bassett
Peter van Schie
Peter Ward
Phenry3@phenry3.com
Phil "Heisenberg" Simon
Phil Borgnes
Phil Correia
Phil Shapiro
Philipp V.W. Grunwald
Philippe Chabot
Phillip D Gonzales
Phillip Smith
Phineas & Jacob
Phoenix Zoellick
Pierce Nichols
Pierre Lempérière
Pietro Conforto Bardellini
Piotr Durlej
PK
Povl Eller
Prashant Agarwal
Priscilla Woolworth
Prudence

PT Bumi Salihara
(Yoga Prakasa)
Purgatos
Quezia Cleto
R. Maxwell
R. R. Atkinson
Rachael Walker
Rachel Castle Herzer
Rachel Clark
Rachel Lovinger
Rajat Ghai
Ramona Hutton-Howe
Randal A Dahl
Raphael Fink
Ray Steele
Rebecca Hempen
Reena Esmail
Rees Maxwell
René Cáceres Reséndiz
Renee Perry
Rennie LeDuc
Reny Barahona
Rev. Darrien Woomer
Ricardo "Rico" Acosta
Rich Peterson
Rich Shumaker
Rich Sommer
Richard Hough
Richard Lewis
Richard Lotz
Richard Melo
Richard Szeto
Rick Wilhelm
rlh
RM Garretson
Rob @baconbaum
Felberbaum
Rob Mills

Rob Mizell

Rob Neal

Rob Nolten

Rob Portil

Robert Belton

Robert Iken Lee

Robert Ristroph

Robert Riteco

Robert Sheff

Robert Spiropoulos

Robert St-Jacques

Robert Thuston

Roberto Greco

Roberto Rosario

Robin Hunicke

Robin Kromann

robosnake

Rodney Hill

Rodrigo Ortiz Vinholo

Rohit Ramesh

Romain Bazile

Roman Tsukerman

Ron Lauzon

Rosa O'Driscoll

Roshan Sunil

Roy Liuzza

Ruth Ann Harnisch

Ryan Buckland

Ryan Clark

Ryan Deugan

Ryan E. Freckleton-

Ryan Oclee

Ryan Reiber

S Carter

S Marek

S. C. Versillee

S. Lapeyre

Sacha De'Angeli

Sage Dahlen

Saira Jesani

Sam Lade

Sam van Roon

Samuel Andert

Samuel Basa

Samuel Forbes

Sandra Reeb-Gruber

Sandra Salter

Sanjoy Datta

Sara Hendren

Sara J. Kramer

Sara Marie Korn

Sara Moffat

Sara Thompson &
    Mark Lindner

Sarah Barthelet

Sarah E. Collins

Sarah Hooge

Sarah Simpson

Sarah Szalavitz

Sasha Gelzin

Sasha Irby

SB

Scott A.G. Nelson

Scott Bratcher

Scott Burau

Scott Dutcher

Scott Henshaw

Scott Jones

Scott Kreger

Scott M Collison

Scott McCray

Scott McIntosh

Scott Perlman

Scott Pickard

Scott Woolsey Biggart

Sean Akers

Sean Welsh

Sebastian Ong

Sebastian Orr

Serena Andrews

Serene Ow

Sergey Kiselev

seth godin

Seth Gover

Seth W. Klein

Seumas Macdonald

Shaheen Savarnejad

Shaneque Downie

Shannon Walker

Sharina McCants

Sharjeel Aziz (Shaji)

Sharon Perez

Shaun Farrar

Shayna Gentiluomo

Sherri Wasserman

Shiau-Wei Chew

ShimmerGeek

Shyam Pillai

Siddharth Vanchinathan

Simona Ocelkova

Sir Tedder, Esq.

Sjoerd Adding

Skaja & Sam Wills

Skillshare

Skip Frizzell

Skybur

Smriti Keshari

Sommar Dodge

Sonya Micheals

sophie hwang

Spencer Lambert

Stacey Cournoyer

Stacie Humpherys //
    girl*in*gear studio

Stan Hudecki

Stefan Broda

Stefan Friedli

Stefan Heinz

Stefan Oppl

Stefan Schoenweiss

Steffan Antonas

Steffen Seitz

Stephanie Ard

Stephanie Kalfus

Stephanie King

Stephen Angell

Stephen Bruckert

Stephen in Miami Beach

Steve Garfield

Steve Hurlock

Steve Isaacs

Steve Johnson

Steve MS

Steve Pien

Steve Yao

Steven Dee

Steven List

Steven Yau

Stuart Black

Stuart McDow

Suraj Gupta

Sure

Suri Chen

Susan Bennerstrom

Susan Guevara

Susan Kapuscinski
    Gaylord

Susan Kish

Susan Skoog

Suzanne Fischer

swampfiend

swes87

Tabi Joy
Talya Seligman
Tamara Christensen
Tami Evnin
Tammy MoJo
TAN KWANG CHIAT
TANYA ILARDE
Tappi Honkavaara
Tara Lawrence
Tari
Tarjote Chaggar
Tarmo Toikkanen
Tatiana Jimenez
Tayvid
Ted Brown
Ted Muenster
Ted Trent
Teng Chea
Teri Solow
Terry Carroll-Beyak
Terry S McMahon
Tessa Blake
Tetsuji Asakawa
Thomas Banakas
Thomas Shepard
Tieg Zaharia
TigerLily Cross
Tim Burnett
Tim Densham
Tim Hackbarth
Tim Maly
Timothy R. Armstrong
Tina Hanke
TJ McCue
TL
Todd Lemoine
Todd Sahba
TODOR ILIEV

Tolulope Bukola
Tom Elia
tom evans
Tom Jenkins
Tom Parker
Tom Stacey
Tomasz Finc
Tooth fairy
Torben Olander
Travis Cox
Tredesigns.com
Trevor Brummitt
Tricia Somma
Tristan Price
Trysh Travis
Twilla Coates
Ty Liang
UntzUntz WakaTaka Untz
Usaf Alcodray
Vaibhav Bhawsar
Valia Guzman-Fischer
Varud Gupta
Vasil Kolev
Vicky
Victor A. Bernacé
Victor Mota
Victoria Wasson Pueschel
Victorious Rodriguez
Viktor Solt-Bittner
Vilhelm Rothe
Vin Dang
Vivien Leung
Ward Vandebrouck
Wayne from Maine
Wayne Wilson
wendy macnaughton
Wendy S. Dirr
Werner Schmid-Barnden

Wes Baker
Wickedly Wanda (Pilié)
    from Montreal
WilFromTheFutr
Will Foy
Will Gowen
Will Jones
Will McGregor
Will Selling
William Bettridge-
    Radford
William Logan
William Payne
William Ward
Winston Yu
Wolfgang Nibori
Wolfgang Schuster
Xavier Belanche Alonso
Yaqoubs
Yehuda Miller
yene
Yes
Yoh Sato
Yusuf Abdi
Yvonne Huiskamp-Ung
Yvonne L.
Zabrina Way
Zach Coulter
Zachariah Willoh
Zachary Fannin
Zachary Kyritsis
Zack Armstrong
Zan Chandler
Zev Steen
Zishu Chen
Zoë Jackson

DON'T GO BACK TO SCHOOL

About the author

 Kio Stark is a writer, teacher, grad school dropout, and independent learning activist. Her first novel, *Follow Me Down*, was published in 2011. Stark teaches at NYU's graduate Interactive Telecommunications Program and coordinates the Knight-Mozilla OpenNews learning initiative. Some of the things she's taught herself include how to develop and print photos, novel writing, the psychology and neuroscience of delusions, and the history of art theft and forgery. She talks to strangers and is notorious for opening doors that say "Do Not Enter."